A SERVANT'S *Heart*

180 ENCOURAGING
THOUGHTS FOR
CHURCH VOLUNTEERS

TIFFANY
ROSS

An Imprint of Barbour Publishing, Inc.

Member of the
Evangelical Christian
Publishers Association

Contents

PART ONE

♡

Called to Care

1
Every Life Matters

So God created mankind in his own image, in the image of God he created them; male and female he created them.
GENESIS 1:27

Your life counts.

You are a one-of-a-kind masterpiece, the very workmanship of God (Ephesians 2:10), knit together in your mother's womb, fearfully and wonderfully made (Psalm 139:13–14). Indeed, the very hairs of your head are all numbered by the Lord—that's how precious you are to Him (Luke 12:7).

And if you have faith as small as a mustard seed, nothing will be impossible for you (Matthew 17:20). You can do all things through Christ who strengthens you (Philippians 4:13).

So if God is for you, who can be against you (Romans 8:31)?

Take a moment to thank Jesus for His many blessings. Pray something like this:

O Lord Jesus, I praise You and thank You for giving me life here on earth and for all eternity. I thank You for making my life count, for giving me purpose and meaning. And so I pray the very words of the psalmist David: "Praise the LORD, my soul; all my inmost being, praise his holy name. Praise the LORD, my soul, and forget not all his benefits—who forgives all your sins and heals all your diseases" (Psalm 103:1–3).

2

Every Heart Aches

For all have sinned and fall short of the glory of God.
ROMANS 3:23

We all have a deadly "virus" in our hearts. As we grow, the illness gradually takes over, poisoning our thoughts, twisting our actions, and preventing us from living the lives God wants for us. It keeps our faith walk weak and bedridden instead of healthy and thriving.

This deadly condition, of course, is *sin*.

This isn't a new problem. Paul lamented in his letter to the Romans: "There's nobody living right, not even one, nobody who knows the score, nobody alert for God. They've all taken the wrong turn; they've all wandered down blind alleys. No one's living right; I can't find a single one. Their throats are gaping graves, their tongues slick as mudslides. Every word they speak is tinged with poison. They open their mouths and pollute the air. They race for the honor of sinner-of-the-year, litter the land with heartbreak and ruin, don't know the first thing about living with others. They never give God the time of day" (Romans 3:10–18 MSG).

But there's hope.

Jesus—the Great Physician—invites every man, woman, and child to receive the only cure. Have you and your loved ones accepted it? Do you trust Him as your Lord and Savior? He reminds us in Mark 2:17: "It is not the healthy who need a doctor, but the sick. I have not come to call the righteous, but sinners."

3

Jesus Is the Answer

"I am the way and the truth and the life.
No one comes to the Father except through me."
JOHN 14:6

In spite of our stubborn hearts and sinful condition, the Lord won't give up on any of us—*ever*. But He won't force us to believe either.

Max Lucado reminds us that the choice is ours: "God will whisper. He will shout. He will touch and tug. He will take away our burdens; He'll even take away our blessings. If there are a thousand steps between us and Him, He will take all but one. But He will leave the final one for us."[1]

Have you taken that final step? Are you committed to helping your family and friends take that step, too? Trusting Jesus as our Lord and Savior is the most important decision we'll ever make, because He is the *only* answer to our sin dilemma.

The death and resurrection of our Lord is what frees a believer from sin, not an act of their own will. By faith, we daily turn our lives over to the One who has given us new life. The apostle Paul emphasizes Jesus' amazing gift of salvation in Philippians 2:8: "And being found in appearance as a man, he humbled himself by becoming obedient to death—even death on a cross!"

---

1. Max Lucado, *God's Promises for You* (Nashville: Thomas Nelson, Inc., 2006), p. 171.

4

Believers Are Forgiven and Free

*In him we have redemption through his blood, the forgiveness
of sins, in accordance with the riches of God's grace that he
lavished on us with all wisdom and understanding.*

EPHESIANS 1:7–8

Even though Christ-followers wrestle with sin, we are no longer slaves to it. We are forgiven and free, and we have new identities in Christ. "Do not offer any part of yourself to sin as an instrument of wickedness, but rather offer yourselves to God as those who have been brought from death to life; and offer every part of yourself to him as an instrument of righteousness. For sin shall no longer be your master, because you are not under the law, but under grace" (Romans 6:13–14).

According to Paul, we must continually "put off" or "put away" the characteristics of our old life and "put on" characteristics of our new life. (See Ephesians 4:22–32.) Erwin W. Lutzer admits that this process take loads of patience *and* discipline—qualities many of us can improve upon in our lives. "There are many ways to fail in the Christian life," he says. "But all of them begin with lack of discipline, a conscious decision to take the easy route. Paul says, 'I discipline my body and bring it under control.' The lie is that the body cannot be disciplined, for indeed it can, especially with the help of the Holy Spirit, who gives us self-control."[2]

Are you finding strength through the Holy Spirit to put off your old life? Is the Lord helping you grow in your new one?

---

2. Erwin W. Lutzer, *Your Eternal Reward* (Chicago: Moody Press, © 1998). 58.

5

Eyewitness Encounter: "Blessed By Those Who Give"

Sitting down, Jesus called the Twelve and said, "Anyone who wants to be first, he must be the very last, and the servant of all."
MARK 9:35

Roy and Gail were new to our church. A couple of weeks before Christmas, they stopped by my office for a friendly visit, and Gail handed me a long, rectangular package. She explained that it was a nice, brand-new cane—still in the original box—and she wanted to give it to someone who needed it.

Immediately I thought of an older gentleman named Jim. His health and mobility was declining rapidly because of Parkinson's disease. This once strong and fiercely independent boat repairman now struggled with basic day-to-day tasks, like standing and walking. Yet he was determined to attend church faithfully.

"Yes," I said to the couple, "there's a man in our church who I think could really use this."

On Christmas Day, Jim enthusiastically unwrapped a new cane, which quickly became his most prized possession. Grinning from ear to ear and walking everywhere, it was as if he had a new lease on life.

When I heard how much the cane had blessed Jim's life, I couldn't help shedding some tears of joy. I immediately shared the blessing with the kindhearted gift givers, Roy and Gail.

"You made my day!" Gail exclaimed. "We truly wanted to help someone."

Generosity. It blesses those who give as much (or perhaps more) as it blesses those who receive. Let's be generous today.

—**Kyle, Senior Pastor**

6

Spiritual Nudge:
Madeline L'Engle on Helping Them See God

*Many, Lord my God, are the wonders you have done, the things
you planned for us. None can compare with you; were I to speak
and tell of your deeds, they would be too many to declare.*

PSALM 40:5

The Virgin Birth has never been a major stumbling block in my struggle
with Christianity; it's far less mind-boggling than the power of all creation
stooping so low as to become one of us. But I find myself disturbed at the
changing, by some committee or other, of the "myth" that brought God
and the human creature together in marvelous at-one-ment, as Jacob's
ladder brought heaven and earth together. That's the wonder that God
can reach out and become one with that which has been created.[3]

7

Bible Wisdom: Christ on Serving

FROM MATTHEW 25:40–46

"The King will reply, 'I tell you the truth, whatever you did for one of the
least of these brothers and sisters of mine, you did for me.'

"Then he will say to those on his left, 'Depart from me, you who are
cursed, into the eternal fire prepared for the devil and his angels. For I

---

3. Madeleine L'Engle, *A Stone for a Pillow* (Wheaton, Ill.: Harold Shaw Publishers, 1986),
107-8.

was hungry and you gave me nothing to eat, I was thirsty and you gave me nothing to drink, I was a stranger and you did not invite me in, I needed clothes and you did not clothe me, I was sick and in prison and you did not look after me.'

"They also will answer, 'Lord, when did we see you hungry or thirsty or a stranger or needing clothes or sick or in prison, and did not help you?'

"He will reply, 'Truly I tell you, whatever you did not do for one of the least of these, you did not do for me.'

"Then they will go away to eternal punishment, but the righteous to eternal life."

8

Salvation Is a Gift to Be Shared

For it is by grace you have been saved, through faith—
and this is not from yourselves, it is the gift of God.
EPHESIANS 2:8

Through Jesus, we can know truth and receive the gift of salvation. But in order to receive it, we must first understand that we need it.

C.S. Lewis explained our need for understanding this way: "Christianity tells people to repent and promises them forgiveness. It therefore has nothing (as far as I know) to say to people who do not know that they have anything to repent of and who do not feel that they need forgiveness. It is after you have realized that there is a real Moral Law, and a Power behind that law, and that you have broken that law and put yourself wrong with that Power—it is after all this, and not a moment sooner, that Christianity begins to talk."[4]

Think about the people around you who don't even realize that they

---

4. C.S. Lewis, *Mere Christianity*, (San Francisco: Harper San Francisco, © 1952, C.S. Lewis Pte. Ltd.), 32.

need a Savior. For them, Christianity is silent. Are you ready to make your faith "talk"? Salvation is a gift to be shared. Be bold, be generous, and spread the Good News to everyone you meet.

9

Invite Them to Join the Party

He will swallow up death forever. The Sovereign Lord will wipe away the tears from all faces; he will remove his people's disgrace from all the earth.
ISAIAH 25:8–9

For most of us, dying is the furthest thing from our minds. But at some point we all need to ask ourselves some important questions about death: "If I died tomorrow, would I go to heaven?" "Is death the end?" "How will I deal with the inevitable loss of those I love so much? Will they have eternal life?"

No one is immortal. Someday, whether by accident or illness or old age, each one of us will die. Death stings. It's an enemy of both God and man. But if you're a Christian, you know that your final heartbeat isn't really the end. And when you stand at the graveside of a Christian brother or sister, you know your loss is only temporary. When you and other believers meet Jesus face to face, it will be the grand beginning to a life that never ends—the ultimate homecoming.

God doesn't want anyone to miss out on eternal life with Him, so the desire to witness should captivate every servant's heart. Are you willing to speak up? Invite someone to God's eternal party!

10

Heaven Is Our Future Home

For here we do not have an enduring city,
but we are looking for the city that is to come.
HEBREWS 13:14

Think of—
Stepping on shore, and finding it Heaven!
Of taking hold of a hand, and finding it God's hand.
Of breathing a new air, and finding it celestial air.
Of feeling invigorated, and finding it immortality.
Of passing from storm to tempest to an unbroken calm.
Of waking up, and finding it Home.[5]

We are free to follow a life-path that will lead us to His eternal kingdom (a place that promises to be far greater than Eden). . .or we can remain in the thorns. We can choose life by the spirit and work into our hearts the qualities of God: *love, joy, peace, patience, kindness, goodness, faithfulness, gentleness, self-control.* Or we can choose to act on our sinful nature and allow ourselves to degenerate with cravings of the flesh: *sexual immorality, impurity, debauchery, idolatry, hatred, discord, jealousy, fits of rage, selfish ambition, dissensions, factions, envy, drunkenness.* (See also Galatians 5:16–26).

Heaven is our future home. So in this life, let's choose the path that leads to eternity with God, and let's help others find it, too.

---

5. Author Unknown, "Heaven," in *Best Loved Poems of the American People,* sel. Hazel Fellman (New York: Doubleday, © 1965), 331.

11
God's Heirs Must Always Care

*Now if we are children, then we are heirs—heirs of God
and co-heirs with Christ, if indeed we share in his
sufferings in order that we may also share in his glory.*
ROMANS 8:17

Charles H. Spurgeon, one of the greatest and most popular preachers
in nineteenth-century England, asked Christians some hard-hitting
questions: "What have you been doing with your life? Is Christ living in
your home and yet you have not spoken to him for months? Do not let
me condemn you or judge; only let your conscience speak: Have we not
all lived too much without Jesus? Have we not grown content with the
world to the neglect of Christ?"[6]

We are God's heirs, and so we must live like it. Even today Jesus
calls out to people, "Follow Me!" Those who are wise listen and—
without hesitation—leave their old ways behind. They find in Christ
a new direction, a new purpose, a new identity—an amazing new life.
They discover real adventure, true fulfillment—and ultimate love. Not
the kind of love that originates on earth, but the kind that is perfect; the
kind that is unconditional and unlimited.

---

6. Spurgeon, Charles H., *Spiritual Revival, The Want of the Church,* in *Devotional Classics:
Selected Readings for Individuals and Groups,* comp. Richard Foster and James Bryan Smith
(San Francisco: Harper San Francisco, © 1993), pp. 333-34.

12

Eyewitness Encounter: "The Extraordinary Ordinary"

When morning came, he called his disciples to him and chose twelve of them, whom he also designated apostles: Simon (whom he named Peter), his brother Andrew, James, John, Philip, Bartholomew, Matthew, Thomas, James son of Alphaeus, Simon who was called the Zealot, Judas son of James, and Judas Iscariot, who became a traitor.

LUKE 6:13–16

"Hey, Bible Boy. Where's your Word?" shouted a voice from across the crowded hall.

Fifteen-year-old Eric grinned and held up a tattered book with fluorescent lime-green words—HOLY BIBLE—handwritten across the cover.

"Right here," he said. "Wouldn't leave home without it!"

It was a Monday morning at a Fort Walton Beach, Florida, high school, and Eric loved his new reputation. While other guys returned from the weekend bragging about how much they drank, Eric couldn't stop boasting about his awesome God. . .and the amazing eternal adventure we can have through Jesus Christ.

"This world needs bold Christians," Eric told me during a phone conversation. (When I heard about this teen's extraordinary witness, I had to learn more.) "We need teenagers who are willing to stand in the face of what's popular and say, 'Jesus is the *only* truth, the *only* life, and the *only* way.'

"As far as being rejected, I don't want to stand before God on Judgment Day and hear the words, 'I counted on you to tell your friends about Me, but you didn't.'

"I don't want my friends to spend eternity in hell. I can't be selfish.

I've got to speak up. . .and do my part to change my school for Christ. So I started a lunch-hour Bible study, and today, I'm not the only Bible Boy at school—there's a lot of us now!"

We should all be following in Eric's footsteps: taking Jesus to work, to our neighborhoods, to the lost corners of this world. He is proving that seemingly ordinary steps can lead to an extraordinary impact for Christ.

—**Michael, Youth Worker**

13

Spiritual Nudge: Henry T. Blackaby on God-Sized Assignments

The Lord had said to Abram, "Go from your country,
people and your father's household to the land I will show you.
I will make you into a great nation, and I will bless you;
I will make your name great, and you will be a blessing.
I will bless those who bless you, and whoever curses you I will
curse; and all peoples on earth will be blessed through you."
GENESIS 12:1–3

"I have come to the place in my life that, if the assignment I sense God is giving me is something that I know I can handle, I know it probably is not from God. The kind of assignments God gives in the Bible are God-sized. They are always beyond what people can do, because He wants to demonstrate His nature, His strength, His provision, and His kindness by His people and to a watching world. That is the only way the world will come to know Him."

14

Bible Wisdom: Christ on the Lord's Prayer

From Matthew 6:5–15

"And when you pray, do not be like the hypocrites, for they love to pray standing in the synagogues and on the street corners to be seen by others. Truly I tell you, they have received their reward in full. But when you pray, go into your room, close the door and pray to your Father, who is unseen. Then your Father, who sees what is done in secret, will reward you. And when you pray, do not keep on babbling like pagans, for they think they will be heard because of their many words. Do not be like them, for your Father knows what you need before you ask him.

"This, then, is how you should pray:

> *'Our Father in heaven,*
> *hallowed be your name,*
> *your kingdom come,*
> *your will be done*
> *on earth as it is in heaven.*
> *Give us today our daily bread.*
> *And forgive us our debts,*
> *as we also have forgiven our debtors.*
> *And lead us not into temptation,*
> *but deliver us from the evil one.'*

For if you forgive other people when they sin against you, your heavenly Father will also forgive you. But if you do not forgive others their sins, your Father will not forgive your sins."

15

The World Is Trapped in Darkness

The light shines in the darkness,
but the darkness has not overcome it.
JOHN 1:5

In the tiny mountain town of Pineville, West Virginia, the abundant seams of coal ripple through the landscape. These ancient deposits are treasure to those who mine it. Coal can heat a home and put food on the table. That's how it was for my father, a coal miner named Floyd Cox. With one exception, however...

"Coal is valuable, yet it's not the *real* treasure of life," he was fond of saying. He told this to everyone—from burly miners to the busloads of kids he drove to church on Sunday mornings. "It's not even nearly the most valuable." He'd hold up his Bible. "This is the true treasure."

Floyd was a man who *lived* God's Word. During his seventy-two years on earth, he trusted it, revered it, and was never ashamed to talk about it. As it did for the psalmists, the scriptures illuminated his path— brighter than the headlamp on the hard hat that he wore. And he was committed to leading others into the light of salvation.

Do you share my father's passion for the Gospel? Open your Bible and lead someone to Jesus. "In him was life, and that life was the light of all mankind" (John 1:4).

16

Somebody Needs You

If anyone has material possessions and sees a brother or sister in need but has no pity on them, how can the love of God be in that person?
1 JOHN 3:17

Some Christians have this idea that we're supposed to live our lives in a safe bubble, separated from the rest of the world.

News flash: God wants us to pop our bubbles. He's counting on us to engage the planet for Him—offering acceptance and a listening ear, preparing a hot meal, providing shelter for the homeless. Somebody needs you. More precisely, somebody needs a fresh encounter with the God you serve. "The King will reply, 'Truly I tell you, whatever you did for one of the least of these brothers and sisters of mine, you did for me'" (Matthew 25:40).

So how should you reach out? Begin by telling your story to someone you meet. Share what you're all about, what Christ is all about. Next, let your actions speak love. Be kind, be generous—take a step out of your comfort zone. Invite someone to church, offer a prayer, or share a passage from scripture. The smallest gesture can inspire someone to make a lifelong commitment to Christ.

17

Giving Is Better than Receiving

And do not forget to do good and to share with others,
for with such sacrifices God is pleased.
HEBREWS 13:16

Even if we have 20/20 vision, most of us could use some divine "eye surgery."

We know that our lives could—and *should*—be more Christlike. We know that we're not only supposed to consider our own interests, but also the interests of others. (See Philippians 2:4.) And we usually feel convicted by Jesus' words in Mark 12:31: "Love your neighbor as yourself."

Yet, all too often our focus is on ourselves.

Think about a typical day. Much of it is spent trying to make life work *without* God at the center. But we expect Him to cooperate with us—relating to us on *our* terms, revolving around *our* plans, solving problems so we can live the way *we want to live*. And while we may think our lives are humming along just fine, we are deceived. Gradually, choice by choice, a chasm between us and God grows wider and deeper.

Ready to let God do that divine "eye surgery"? Ask Him to refocus your vision. Ask Him to give you a heart for others—showing you that giving is better than receiving.

18

Be Hospitable to One Another

Each one should use whatever gift you have received to serve others,
as faithful stewards of God's grace in its various forms.
1 PETER 4:10

From His birth to His death on a cross, Jesus' life is a shining example of humility and service. He reached out to those individuals no one else wanted around. He brought love to the unloved, hope to the hopeless. How about you? Ask God to help you find at least one nonbeliever you can reach—through prayer, as well as service.

Take time to look around. Someone needs you—someone at church, at school, at home. There's that seventy-four-year-old man whose wife has Alzheimer's disease. . . He needs someone to talk to. Then there's that couple with a handicapped child. . . They really could use a break. You don't have to head off on a mission trip to Panama to serve God. Do it every day in lots of little ways—like taking the time to talk to that elderly man or volunteering to help that couple with their yard.

Are you using your gifts to serve others?

19

Eyewitness Encounter: "Sharing Our Gifts of the Spirit"

*"My grace is sufficient for you,
for power is made perfect in weakness."*

2 CORINTHIANS 12:9

I am so thankful to be a part of a great church family. We gather together every week to worship God by reading His Word, praising Him with song, and participating in the sacraments. We have a practice of saying, "We receive this blessing, that we might be a blessing" at the conclusion of communion. This may seem like a small thing, but it represents a whole new way of seeing the world. I have learned that when I give myself unconditionally to God, my life is no longer my own. God places His seal of ownership on me through the work of the Holy Spirit. Without Him, my efforts to bring wisdom, understanding, faith, and healing to the world is a feeble undertaking. But the Spirit makes all things possible through Jesus Christ. I desire to serve others because He desires to serve others. He is at work releasing the gifts of the Spirit to the world through me. I do not own these gifts, but He owns me. My hands carry His love, forgiveness, and reconciliation to others. And this process helps me become more and more like Jesus.

—Tess, Health Care Provider

20

Spiritual Nudge:
Billy Graham on Being Salt and Light

"You are the salt of the earth. But if the salt loses its saltiness how can it be made salty again? It is no longer good for anything, except to be thrown out and trampled underfoot. You are the light of the world. A town built on a hill cannot be hidden. Neither do people light a lamp and put it under a bowl. Instead they put it on its stand, and it gives light to everyone in the house. In the same way, let your light shine before others, that they may see your good deeds and glorify your Father in heaven."
MATTHEW 5:13–16

Jesus had the most open and all-encompassing mind that this world has ever seen. His own inner conviction was so strong, so firm, so unswerving that He could afford to mingle with any group secure in the knowledge that He would not be contaminated. It is fear that makes us unwilling to listen to another's point of view, fear that our own ideas may be attacked. Jesus had no such fear, no such pettiness of viewpoint, no need to fence Himself off for His own protection. He knew the difference between graciousness and compromise, and we would do well to learn from Him. He set for us the most magnificent and glowing example of truth combined with mercy of all time, and in departing said: "Go ye and do likewise" (Luke 10:37 KJV).[7]

---

7. Billy Graham, *Unto the Hills* (Nashville: Word Publishing, 1986), 123-4.

21

Bible Wisdom: Christ on Being Prepared for His Return

FROM MARK 13:32–37

"But about that day or hour no one knows, not even the angels in heaven, nor the Son, but only the Father. Be on guard! Be alert! You do not know when that time will come. It's like a man going away: He leaves his house and puts his servants in charge, each with their assigned task, and tells the one at the door to keep watch.

"Therefore keep watch because you do not know when the owner of the house will come back—whether in the evening, or at midnight, or when the rooster crows, or at dawn. If he comes suddenly, do not let him find you sleeping. What I say to you, I say to everyone: 'Watch!'"

22

We Are the Aroma of Christ

For we are to God the pleasing aroma of Christ among those who are being saved and those who are perishing.
2 CORINTHIANS 2:15

What? Me? Walk up to a total stranger in a foreign country, bungle my way through the language barrier, and tell him or her about Jesus Christ? I don't think I can do that!

Bryan couldn't believe what his pastor was asking of him. After all, it was hard enough just being on a summer missions trip, let alone sharing his faith publicly.

"You have nothing to fear," his pastor said with a grin. "Today you are among 'men sent from God,' which means you smell really, really good!"

Bryan sniffed the air and then squinted. "Okay. . .now I'm confused!"

The minister's smile grew even bigger. "It's in the Bible— 2 Corinthians 2:12–17," he explained. "As we share the Good News, Christ 'spreads everywhere the fragrance of the knowledge of Him'— the aroma of eternal life. And we don't have to stress over what to say. The Holy Spirit will give you the *right* words at the *right* moment."

Bryan nodded and took a deep breath. "Glad I smell good," he said. "No worries, no stress. I'll just step out in faith. . ."

As a servant of Jesus Christ, are you speaking "before God with sincerity"? Are you doing your best to share the fragrance of life?

23

We Are Christ's "Letter"

You yourselves are our letter, written on our hearts, known and read by everyone. You show that you are a letter from Christ, the result of our ministry, written not with ink but with the Spirit of the living God, not on tablets of stone but on tablets of human hearts.

2 CORINTHIANS 3:2–3

Christ-followers show their witness one choice at a time.

It's the little things we do every day that reveal if we live for ourselves or for God. And our friends are watching. Actually, they are "reading" our actions. That's exactly what a young lady named Tricia discovered.

When she was in high school, she made a decision to lay down her life for Christ and for her friends, which was hard at first. All around her were different cliques that kids seemed to hide in.

Some looked out for themselves and stepped on whoever they could in order to climb the "popularity ladder." Then there were those who didn't get noticed much—the so-called "losers." But there were a few teens who really tried to make a difference. Those were the kids who Tricia wanted to be like.

So Tricia made an effort to love every person she met, seeing them the way God saw them. Here's what she learned: "When you're authentic and stand up for what you believe, most people will respect you for having confidence, not to mention a backbone. They'll notice that there's something bigger in your life that you live for."

Want to be a strong witness? Be Christ's letter—and let others read your life one choice at a time.

24

We Are Servants of One Another

You, my brothers and sisters, were called to be free. But do not use your freedom to indulge the flesh; rather, serve one another humbly in love.
GALATIANS 5:13

Armed with hammers and paintbrushes, a battalion of four hundred and eight teens and youth workers invaded Greenbrier County, West Virginia. Their mission: spend a week refurbishing more than sixty homes in this mountain community.

Just outside a rickety trailer house, a teen named Brian began playing ball with a five-year-old boy. "I want to help this child have a better place to live," the seventeen-year-old said. "This is why I'm here—for him."

In the process of sprucing up this boy's house, Brian and his church friends were serving the community and building a much stronger foundation—the Gospel. "At each work site, we get a chance to build relationships with the people we serve," says seventeen-year-old Jeff. "We tell them about our Savior. They not only hear our words, but they also see our actions. And that's one of the best ways to spread the Gospel."

Ready to serve your community? Proverbs 3:28 tells us, "Do not say to your neighbor, 'Come back tomorrow and I'll give it to you'—when you already have it with you." Gather the troops from your church and share Christ's love through a work and witness program.

25

We Are Servants of the Lord

Whatever you do, work at it with all your heart, as working for the Lord, not for human masters, since you know that you will receive an inheritance from the Lord as a reward. It is the Lord Christ you are serving.
COLOSSIANS 3:23–24

The Bible instructs us to serve Jesus with all our heart, regardless of the size of the assignment or the amount of recognition we'll receive.

So the countless meals you've dished up during church potlucks and the endless hours you've spent volunteering in the nursery are every bit as important to God as the big, public ministry activities—especially if they're done for Christ's glory.

As we faithfully and consistently serve the Lord, our attitude becomes more and more like His. "Do nothing out of selfish ambition or vain conceit. Rather, in humility value others above yourselves, not looking to your own interests but each of you to the interests of the others" (Philippians 2:3–4).

Who are you serving for Christ's sake? You are His hands and feet;

you speak His words and show His face to those in your care. Are you working with all your heart—for His glory?

26

Eyewitness Encounter: "Tips on Serving the Church"

Therefore, as we have opportunity, let us do good to all people, especially to those who belong to the family of believers.
GALATIANS 6:10

Do you ever overthink a passage of scripture? I do it all the time. I'll look at a verse and try to gather as much information about it as I can. I try to place it into the proper cultural setting and attempt to see what the author was really trying to get across with the verse. What is the true meaning of the passage? Am I interpreting it correctly? I often find myself going back to read the verse or passage more than once. In the end, I usually give up on my analysis. Sometimes the best thing to do is just read what the verse says.

Galatians 6:10 is one of those verses for me. I could read into the verse and think about its context, or I could just read it and follow what it says. It's really plain and simple when I don't overthink it. Do good to everyone, especially to those who are part of God's family. Jesus calls us to love one another. Don't overthink it, just do it.

—Trent, Associate Pastor

27

Spiritual Nudge: Paul on Imitating Christ's Humility

FROM PHILIPPIANS 2:1–11

If you have any encouragement from being united with Christ, if any comfort from his love, if any common sharing in the Spirit, if any tenderness and compassion, then make my joy complete by being like-minded, having the same love, being one in spirit and of one mind. Do nothing out of selfish ambition or vain conceit. Rather, in humility value others better than yourselves, not looking to your own interests but each of you to the interests of others.

In your relationships with one another, have the same mindset as Christ Jesus:

> *Who, being in very nature God,*
> *did not consider equality with God something to be used to his own advantage;*
> *rather, he made himself nothing*
> *by taking the very nature of a servant,*
> *being made in human likeness.*
> *And being found in appearance as a man,*
> *he humbled himself*
> *by becoming obedient to death—*
> *even death on a cross!*
> *Therefore God exalted him to the highest place*
> *and gave him the name that is above every name,*
> *that at the name of Jesus every knee should bow,*
> *in heaven and on earth and under the earth,*
> *and every tongue acknowledge that Jesus Christ is Lord,*
> *to the glory of God the Father.*

28

Bible Wisdom: Christ on His Role as a Servant

FROM MARK 10:42–45

"You know that those who are regarded as rulers of the Gentiles lord it over them, and their high officials exercise authority over them. Not so with you. Instead, whoever wants to become great among you must be your servant, and whoever wants to be first must be slave of all. For even the Son of Man did not come to be served, but to serve, and to give his life as a ransom for many."

29

My Prayer of Intercession: Acting on Behalf of Others

For this reason, ever since I heard about your faith in the Lord Jesus and your love for all God's people, I have not stopped giving thanks for you, remembering you in my prayers. I keep asking that the God of our Lord Jesus Christ, the glorious Father, may give you the Spirit of wisdom and revelation, so that you may know him better. I pray also that the eyes of your heart may be enlightened in order that you may know the hope to which he has called you, the riches of his glorious inheritance in his holy people, and his incomparably great power for us who believe.

EPHESIANS 1:15–19

Intercession means praying on behalf of someone else. The person you intercede for may be incapable of praying on their own. Perhaps they are unconscious—someone who has been in an accident and is undergoing surgery, for example. Maybe they are spiritually lost and simply don't acknowledge God.

When we intercede for others, we draw close to Christ's heart—actually joining Him in prayer. In heaven, Jesus is our High Priest who intercedes with the Father for all of humankind.

Intercessory prayer can be specific—focused on intimate details of a person's life—or it may be general: praying for a nation or a community. The passage above is an example of Paul interceding for the church at Ephesus. He prayed for God's blessing on the people who worshipped there.

My Prayer of Intercession:

_____

_____

_____

30

My Prayers:
"Lord, Bless My Brothers and Sisters. . ."

*Then you will call on me and come and
pray to me, and I will listen to you.*
JEREMIAH 29:12

My Family:

_____

_____

_____

_____

My Friends:

_____

_____

_____

_____

My Church:

_____

_____

_____

_____

My Workplace:

_____

_____

_____

_____

PART TWO

The Face of a Servant

31

How Children Serve the Church

"See that you do not despise one of these little ones. For I tell you that their angels in heaven always see the face of my Father in heaven."
MATTHEW 18:10

Our children are the future, but we spend so much time instructing and correcting our kids to better prepare them for adulthood that we often fail to recognize the example they set for us. Not only do they freely speak the truth, but they are often uninhibited to share their knowledge of God with their friends. Their faith hasn't been challenged by years of struggle that comes with life. Instead, they are often pure of heart and ready to believe. This is why Jesus said we must come to Him like a child.

We can learn a lot from our kids. Just spend one day in Children's Church and listen to the kids sing praise songs. It will warm your heart. Listen in while a child explains God's love to another child. They get so excited and want to share this joy with others. Kids make a difference in the world. They also remind us to look at the world with fresh eyes and wonderment. When is the last time you stepped back and observed the children around you? What did you learn?

32

Kid-Sized Kingdom-Builders

*"Truly I tell you, anyone who will not receive the kingdom
of God like a little child will never enter it."*
MARK 10:15

We often think of small things when we think of children. Small clothes, small furniture, and small people. They eat small portions, occupy small spaces, and live a very basic life. Their tiny stature can trick us into underestimating them. But Jesus held children in high regard. He points to them as the example of how we are to believe. Kids are totally dependent upon their parents for guidance and love. They come into the world with an untarnished heart ready to love and accept. They believe completely and speak freely. And it is these attributes that Jesus is reaffirming in the Gospel of Mark. He emphasizes that we, too, are to come into our relationship with Him as a child.

When Jesus brought the little child before the crowd to show them how to become the greatest in the kingdom of heaven, He didn't make the child do anything courageous or say anything really intelligent or prove their strength in any way. The child just stood there before Jesus as he was. So no matter how small you feel in the sight of God, have faith that He has called you into His kingdom just as you are.

33

A Child Sets the Example

*"Therefore, whoever takes the lowly position of this
child is the greatest in the kingdom of heaven."*
MATTHEW 18:4

Do you ever worry your heart has gotten hard and jaded? Jesus teaches
us in the Bible how to treasure our children—and also how to come to
Him as a child. Nothing is more humble than the heart of a child. If
you've ever held a newborn babe, you were probably captivated by its
purity, innocence, and vulnerability. That experience can cause even the
hardest heart to melt.

Likewise, when we come to the Father, His heart melts for us.
He opens His arms and tells us to come before Him with the humble,
vulnerable heart of a child, allowing Him to become the Father He
desires to be. His lap is a safe place to grow and become more than we
ever thought we could be.

As a result, we find the compassion to lay down our lives for others.
This is the heart of a servant: one that is so humbled by God's greatness
and love that it overflows into the lives of others. Did you know that
the first step of service begins with surrender? Fall into the Lord's open
arms and let Him sustain you. Are you trying to do it all through your
own strength? "Humble your[self] before the Lord, and he will lift you
up" (James 4:10).

34

"From the Lips of Children. . ."

*"Do you hear what these children are saying?" they asked him.
"Yes," replied Jesus, "have you never read, 'From the lips of
children and infants you, Lord, have called forth your praise'?"*
MATTHEW 21:16

After children learn their first word, it's amazing how quickly they become vocal. In no time at all, they are able to make requests, communicate what's wrong, and freely offer passionate opinions. But in the middle of all their questions and unsolicited advice, there can be a wealth of insight. So the next time a child asks "Why?" take the time to stop and ask yourself the same question. When a child reminds us that we are "not being nice," maybe we should stop and think about how our actions are affecting those around us. And most of all, when a child asks us to pray, we should drop to our knees without hesitation.

When we take the time to see the world through the eyes of a child, we can find fresh new thoughts and ideas that are just waiting to be discovered. When is the last time you took advice from someone significantly younger than yourself? What were the results?

35

Eyewitness Encounter: "Nurture a Child's Faith"

Start children off on the way they should go,
and even when they are old they will not turn from it.
PROVERBS 22:6

I sat on the edge of my seat as my daughter walked to the podium. She seemed confident and casual as she straightened her papers and smiled at the audience. But I knew all of the hours she had prepared for this moment. Her face glowed as she began to speak. This was her first speaking competition as a college student. Her speech was well organized, easy to follow, and her delivery seemed effortless. But the real reason I was moved to tears was the subject of her talk. She chose to write and deliver a talk based on Romans 8. She spoke of the original audience, the meaning of Paul's words, the meaning of *grace*, and how it's still applicable to us today. And she did it with clarity and compassion. I sat there and reminisced about all those nights of bedtime devotions, Sunday school lessons, and conversations in the car. All those moments coalesced as my child stood in front of a crowd and delivered the Word of God. All of our intentional efforts had been worthwhile.

There is a reason we are instructed to teach our children about God. Even when it seems like they are not paying attention, the message is getting through. It just may take years for it to show.

—**Julie, Mother**

36

Spiritual Nudge: J.C. Carlile on the Children's Jesus

Behold, children are a heritage from the LORD, the fruit of the womb a reward. Like arrows in the hand of a warrior are the children of one's youth. Blessed is the man who fills his quiver with them! He shall not be put to shame when he speaks with his enemies in the gate.

PSALM 127:3–5 ESV

How good to know that there is a Friend for little children above the bright blue sky, and that He is not only there, wherever that may be, but is with us among the children wherever we are. He has not changed, He is the same yesterday, today and forever. The love-light in His eye as He took the children into His arms has not dimmed. His attraction for the little people is unabated. He still calls them to Himself and blessed are they who come to His feet. Happy are the mothers who bring their little ones to the Savior. If it be true that Heaven lies about us in our infancy, it is surely when the unsophisticated eyes look up into the face that never grows old.[8]

---

8. J.C. Carlile, *Portraits of Jesus Drawn by Himself* (London: Religious Tract Society, n.d.), 90.

37

Bible Wisdom:
Christ on Who Is the Greatest

FROM MARK 9:33–37

They came to Capernaum. When he was in the house, he asked them, "What were you arguing about on the road?" But they kept quiet because on the way they had argued about who was the greatest.

Sitting down, Jesus called the Twelve and said, "Anyone who wants to be first must be the very last, and the servant of all."

He took a little child whom he placed among them. Taking the child in his arms, he said to them, "Whoever welcomes one of these little children in my name welcomes me; and whoever welcomes me does not welcome me but the one who sent me."

38

How Teens and Young Adults Serve the Church

Don't let anyone look down on you because you are young,
but set an example for the believers in speech,
in conduct, in love, in faith and in purity.

1 TIMOTHY 4:12

You can't judge a book by its cover. It's an age-old colloquialism that still rings true. Yet we often believe that young people have everything to learn from us and nothing to teach us in return. Sure, the scriptures are clear that only those who are mature in their faith should be put into leadership positions. But this is no reason to treat the young with dishonor and indifference, because the Lord is clearly able to use them in powerful ways. We are to "come as a child" afterall, aren't we?

When you see someone serving the Lord, loving the Lord, and working alongside you for the Lord, it is your responsibility to build that person up in love and prayer. Our brothers and sisters in Christ come in all shapes, sizes, and ages. And sometimes we can learn a lot from a fresh young perspective. So speak to young people with encouraging words that uplift—especially to those in their teen years who are still finding their identity in Christ as they navigate a challenging and confusing world. They need you. Do you have a teen in your life that needs your encouragement today?

39

Why Every Paul Needs a Timothy

To Timothy my true son in the faith: Grace, mercy and
peace from God the Father and Christ Jesus our Lord.
1 TIMOTHY 1:2

Timothy was a young guy. But he has gone down in history as a man of God who played an instrumental role in the development of the early Church. Most folks who grow up going to church have heard the stories of Peter and Paul. Their missionary efforts after the resurrection of Christ helped spread the Word to places far beyond their own land. And Timothy was right there with them. He was Paul's apprentice who shared the Good News with many. And this is the perfect example of how the church continues from generation to generation. Young people grow up to be leaders and trainers. And they, in turn, train the next group of young leaders. Without the Timothys of the world, the Church would have died out after the first century. Do you have a Timothy in your life? Are you investing in his or her future?

40

What God Expects from Young Servants

In the same way, you who are younger, submit yourselves to your elders. All of you, clothe yourselves with humility toward one another, because, "God opposes the proud but shows favor to the humble."

1 PETER 5:5

Submission. Humility. Self-control. This is what the Lord asks of His followers. A daunting request for a young person who is full of energy and excitement to take on the world. The ways of the Lord can seem like a wet blanket that is being thrown down to dampen their fire. Submission, humilty, and self-control sound a lot like a list of rules that are designed to constrict us into conformity. But the opposite is the case. These godly traits pave the way to knowing Him better and reaping the benefits of His freedom and grace. And God desires for all of His people to grow closer to Him every day, living bold lives that are directed by the Holy Spirit. Young servants of Jesus can reach a generation that adults cannot. But an undisciplined youth is like buckshot exploding in all directions—though well-intentioned, their energies often miss the mark. But a young, disciplined, humble servant with self-control is a force to be reckoned with. How can you help a young servant find excitement in the ways of the Lord?

41

Greatness Starts Young

He did what was right in the eyes of the LORD and followed the ways of his father David, not turning aside to the right or to the left.
2 CHRONICLES 34:2

Mozart debuted his musical talents at the age of four. Andrew Bynum played his first NBA game at age eighteen. LeAnn Rimes won a Grammy at age fourteen. Aelita Andrea began painting at age two. Mark Zuckerberg created Facebook while he was in college. Young people and their talents have always had an impact on the world. David, Timothy, and Esther are all biblical examples of godly young men and women who contributed to the kingdom of God.

The Church is comprised of people of all ages and abilities. And we are called to encourage and incorporate everyone into the body. People don't have to wait until they are older and wiser to be a part of God's mission. Actually, some roles are better suited for younger folks. The zeal, excitement, and freedom of youth can be very appealing to some people. We need to help these individuals plug in to the larger mission as they explore their identity and abilities. Are we helping folks find their place in the Kingdom—regardless of their age? Are we seeking out greatness in our youngest members?

42

Eyewitness Encounter: "When Youth Honor Their Elders"

"Stand up in the presence of the aged, show respect for the elderly and revere your God. I am the LORD."

LEVITICUS 19:32

Anytime my mother couldn't find me playing among my group of friends, she would call Mrs. Barber. I'd usually be sitting on her porch or inside her home talking with that dear elderly lady. We both cherished our time together.

I've always loved older people. I love to hear their stories, their wisdom. I still have a great relationship with all four of my grandparents today. A recent conversation with my maternal grandmother brought one of the best compliments: "I like talking to you. You're good at talking to old people. We don't push each other. You're easy to talk to."

I don't take that compliment lightly. It's rare to find real-life, intergenerational interaction and meaningful conversation. I truly feel that growing up in a small coal camp in West Virginia, being taught that everyone has value, and spending so much of my "play" time with Mrs. Barber taught me to show respect for the aged. It's not enough to simply sit in a room with them in librarylike silence. Our elders have much to teach us if we only take the time to listen as they retell the chapters of their lives and inscribe their wisdom upon our hearts. God commands it.

—**Amy, District Children's Director**

43

Spiritual Nudge: Alex and Brett Harris on Doing "Hard Things"

*Lead me in Your truth and teach me, for You are
the God of my salvation; on You I wait all the day.*
PSALM 25:5 NKJV

We believe our generation is ready for a change. Ready for something that doesn't promise a whole new life if you'll just buy the right pair of jeans or use the right kind of deodorant. We believe our generation is ready to rethink what young people are capable of doing and becoming. And we've noticed that once wrong ideas are debunked and cleared away, our generation is quick to choose a better way, even if it's also more difficult.

We've seen this idea transform average teenagers into world-changers able to accomplish incredible things. And they started by simply being willing to break the mold of what society thinks teens are capable of.

We're not telling you to do pointless hard things just because they are hard. And if you're a Christian, we're certainly not telling you that if you work harder or make yourself uncomfortable on purpose, God will love you more. He will never—could never—love you any more than He does right now.

So that's what we're not doing. What we are doing is challenging people our age to grab hold of a more exciting option for their youth than the one portrayed as normal in society today.[9]

---

9. Alex and Brett Harris, "Against the Flow: Choose to Do Hard Things," August 2008, *Breakaway* magazine, 29-30.

44

Bible Wisdom: Christ on Narrow Gates and Good Fruit

FROM MATTHEW 7:13–23

"Enter through the narrow gate. For wide is the gate and broad is the road that leads to destruction, and many enter through it. But small is the gate and narrow the road that leads to life, and only a few find it.

"Watch out for false prophets. They come to you in sheep's clothing, but inwardly they are ferocious wolves. By their fruit you will recognize them. Do people pick grapes from thornbushes, or figs from thistles? Likewise, every good tree bears good fruit, but a bad tree bears bad fruit. A good tree cannot bear bad fruit, and a bad tree cannot bear good fruit. Every tree that does not bear good fruit is cut down and thrown into the fire. Thus, by their fruit you will recognize them.

"Not everyone who says to me, 'Lord, Lord,' will enter the kingdom of heaven, but only the one who does the will of my Father who is in heaven. Many will say to me on that day, 'Lord, Lord, did we not prophesy in your name and in your name drive out demons and in your name perform many miracles?' Then I will tell them plainly, 'I never knew you. Away from me, you evildoers!' "

45

How Women Serve the Church

*She opens her arms to the poor and
extends her hands to the needy.*
PROVERBS 31:20

In some ways, I'm a typical woman. I am a cook, dedicated mom, landscaper, plumber, tutor, political activist, and Sunday school teacher. And this list is just a sampling of the tasks that I might juggle on any given day. Multitasking is a requirement for any woman who has a family, works, and serves the Lord. The Church is a complex and diverse community, and there are always tasks to be accomplished and lessons to be taught. Many times, a woman's ability to do many things at once is what helps a local church make it through the week. Some may view women as the softer, more compassionate members of the Church. But they also tend to be the ones who provide a strong foundation for so many others in unspoken and unseen ways. So whether the women of your church are speaking, singing, teaching, or silently praying for others, find a way to support them as they serve the Lord. Their dedication is vital to God's mission. When is the last time you said "thank you" to the women in your congregation?

46

One in Christ Jesus

There is neither Jew nor Gentile, neither slave nor free,
nor is there male and female, for you are all one in Christ Jesus.
GALATIANS 3:28

There is an excitement when people are gathered together for a common cause; a synergy in a crowd that you just can't get when you stand alone. There's an energy found at sporting events, political rallies, and concerts that comes from everyone working toward a single goal. There's nothing like it. And the same is true when believers are gathered together to pray, worship, or share testimonies of what the Lord is doing in their lives. Our faith grows exponentially when we come before the Lord together.

It was the same for the disciples as they followed Jesus. When they gathered together and devoted themselves to prayer, it was a mighty exerpience and their lives were changed. Every time, God showed up . . .and He still does. As important as our personal work and service for Him is, it's important to recognize that we were created to live in communion with one another. We are not whole outside of a proper relationship with God and with others. And when we get it right, it is powerful and lasting. How is your community relationship? Is there anything you can do to help build stronger bonds among your fellow believers?

47

Devoted to Prayer

They all joined together constantly in prayer, along with the
women and Mary the mother of Jesus, and with his brothers.
ACTS 1:14

In the wake of Jesus' death, resurrection, and incredible ascension into heaven, His disciples found themselves confused, reeling with emotion, and feeling out of balance. Everything they believed about the Messiah had been blown out of the water. Have you found yourself stunned with disbelief over something that has happened to you in the Church? In such situations, what should we do? We can learn from those who have gone before us. When faced with adversity, they often "continued with one accord in prayer and supplication" (Acts 1:14 KJV). Retreat to your upper room and cry out to God from your secret place. Devote yourself to prayer as you open your heart to Him. Lay everything at the foot of the cross. And stay there until the answer comes, no matter how long it takes. When we follow His lead, He will take us places we never dreamed of.

His power is made perfect in our weakness. He gives us wisdom and strength to move forward in humility as we hold onto Him and His promises. Have you devoted yourself to prayer? Are you allowing Him to lead you into service?

48

Committed to Evangelism

I commend to you our sister Phoebe, a deacon of the church in Cenchreae. I ask you to receive her in the Lord in a way worthy of his people and to give her any help she may need from you, for she has been the benefactor of many people, including me.

ROMANS 16:1–2

In Romans 16, we find a long list of people who were devoted to sharing the Good News with the world. They were a committed people who faced danger and ridicule with joy in their hearts. Paul is writing to encourage them during difficult days. He is offering them advice as they faced prison and persecution of all kinds. In those days, Rome was not friendly to Christians. Their compassion for the less fortunate branded them as an underdeveloped people. They were treated like second-class citizens because they did not subscribe to the selfish mentality of the day. But this did not deter them. They were devoted to spreading the Gospel. In the aftermath of Jesus' ascension, there were some who fell away. But the believers who had a real and genuine encounter with Jesus stood firm. They relied on the direction of His Holy Spirit as they devoted themselves to the mission. And Paul's encouragement is a great example of how we can support each other today. Are you standing firm? Are you helping those around you as they face the difficulties of life?

49

Eyewitness Encounter: "My Mother's Contagious Hospitality"

Sitting down, Jesus called the Twelve and said, "Anyone who wants to be first must be the very last, and the servant of all."
MARK 9:35

My mother grew up the youngest of seven kids. Her family lived in the small town of Glasgow, West Virginia, where her father was an electrician in the coal mines and her mother was a very loving homemaker. My grandmother was always sharing wise words that we later recognized were quotes from Proverbs. One of my favorite memories is when the family would sit around the supper table and chat while we ate. We ate a lot of pinto beans and cornbread, which was a tradition leftover from the depression. With just one bowl and one spoon, we filled our tummies with country food.

Later in life, my mother taught us more about table etiquette and manners. She just knew it would come in handy when we grew up and dined with important people. She didn't want us to embarrass ourselves. But one of the greatest things she taught us was how to welcome people into our home with warmth and hospitality. We hosted ministers, missionaries, evangelists, and many folks from church. The room was always full of stories and laughter as we connected as God's family. All were welcomed and loved. What a great way to show His compassion through an everyday practice of sharing a meal.

—**Rhonda, Pastor's Wife**

50

Spiritual Nudge: Mother Teresa on "Living" God's Kindness

Never let loyalty and faithfulness leave you. Tie them around your neck; write them on the tablet of your heart.

PROVERBS 3:3 HCSB

Spread love everywhere you go: First of all, in your own house. Give love to your children, to your wife or husband, to a next-door neighbor. . . . Let no one ever come to you without leaving better and happier. Be the living expression of God's kindness; kindness in your face, kindness in your eyes, kindness in your smile, kindness in your warm greeting.[10]

51

Bible Wisdom: Christ on Sowing Well

FROM LUKE 8:1–15

After this, Jesus traveled about from one town and village to another, proclaiming the good news of the kingdom of God. The Twelve were with him, and also some women who had been cured of evil spirits and diseases: Mary (called Magdalene) from whom seven demons had come out; Joanna the wife of Chuza, the manager of Herod's household; Susanna; and many others. These women were helping to support them

---

10. John C. Maxwell, *Your Bridge to a Better Future* (Nashville: Thomas Nelson Publishers, 1997), 77.

out of their own means.

While a large crowd was gathering and people were coming to Jesus from town after town, he told this parable: "A farmer went out to sow his seed. As he was scattering the seed, some fell along the path; it was trampled on, and the birds ate it up. Some fell on rocky ground, and when it came up, the plants withered because they had no moisture. Other seed fell among thorns, which grew up with it and choked the plants. Still other seed fell on good soil. It came up and yielded a crop, a hundred times more than was sown."

When he said this, he called out, "Whoever has ears to hear, let them hear."

His disciples asked him what this parable meant. He said, "The knowledge of the secrets of the kingdom of God has been given to you, but to others I speak in parables, so that,

" 'though seeing, they may not see;

though hearing, they may not understand.' "

"This is the meaning of the parable: The seed is the word of God. Those along the path are the ones who hear, and then the devil comes and takes away the word from their hearts, so that they may not believe and be saved. Those on the rocky ground are the ones who receive the word with joy when they hear it, but they have no root. They believe for a while, but in the time of testing they fall away. The seed that fell among thorns stands for those who hear, but as they go on their way they are choked by life's worries, riches and pleasures, and they do not mature. But the seed on good soil stands for those with a noble and good heart, who hear the word, retain it, and by persevering produce a crop."

52

How Men Serve the Church

Be on your guard; stand firm in the faith;
be courageous; be strong. Do everything in love.
1 CORINTHIANS 16:13–14

David sat on the tailgate of the old beat-up pickup truck in the parking lot of the church. He was covered in dirt as he examined the blisters on his hands. He was only fourteen but had volunteered to come work with the men of the church as they repaired the roof and siding of the church building. It had been a long hot day and David was exhausted. He was surprised at how difficult it was to keep up with all the "old guys." Soon he was joined by several of the men as they gathered for some sweet tea. They laughed and told funny stories. As they ended their break, they patted David on the back and gave him a nod of approval. David no longer felt like a young kid who didn't belong. He felt like a part of the group. He had offered what he had, strong young muscles, and the older men had welcomed him.

Working side by side, this multigenerational group of men sets an example of how God has called us all to be a part of His family. They are doing more than fixing the building; what they offer to each other through camaraderie and community is far more significant. They are creating unity through service and acceptance.

53

Shepherds of God's Flock

Be shepherds of God's flock that is under your care, watching over them—not because you must, but because you are willing, as God wants you to be; not pursuing dishonest gain, but eager to serve.

1 PETER 5:2

All those who serve are also leaders, and God has given us the tremendous responsibility of tending His flock. This powerful and humbling charge is how He cares for His people. As a servant-leader, we must strive to find that balance between giving and receiving. Jesus was the ultimate servant-leader. He was confident and humble. He was a seeker and a teacher. He was loving and stern. And all of His actions came from an overwhelming desire to embrace others with love and forgiveness.

It's easy to define ourselves using the standards of power and position. It's how we are perceived in our workplace, at home, and at church. But it's not the way of Christ. Jesus has called us to first humble ourselves before Him. This is where we get our courage and strength. Our relationships point to Christ as we release our desire for power and truly become servants. We should strive to help others mold themselves into servants of the Kingdom by setting a positive example. Are you a servant-leader? Or are you still trying to lead by relying on your own earthly power and authority?

54

Workman Approved by God

Do your best to present yourself to God as one approved,
a worker who does not need to be ashamed and
who correctly handles the word of truth.

2 TIMOTHY 2:15

Who are we working for? Why do we spend so much time volunteering at church? It may be out of tradition, or because that's how we were raised. And sometimes, it's because it makes us feel like we are making a positive impact on our world. But these reasons aren't enough. The reason we serve is because we have been accepted into the family of God and now share in His mission to redeem the world. Our perspective on service to others is dramatically impacted by *why* we serve. If it is just for ourselves, or because we are forced to, in the result will be resentment and frustration.

Second Timothy 2:15 reminds us that we live for a higher purpose. We work for God. And He expects us to work together for His good. Our actions should always begin and end in an effort to please Him. It's good to have goals, but it is almost more important that we accomplish them in ways that are pleasing to Him. He is far more interested in how we live and work together than in any earthly gain on our part. So don't be distracted by difficult people or situations as you serve. Stay focused on God and allow His Spirit to guide your daily steps. Would your actions, today, be approved by God? Does His mission drive your actions?

55

A Royal Priesthood

But you are a chosen people, a royal priesthood, a holy nation,
God's special possession, that you may declare the praises of
him who called you out of darkness into his wonderful light.

1 PETER 2:9

Shepherding is hard work and carries a lot of responsibility. And it has never been a very prestigious position. But it's one that is found throughout scripture. Jesus referred to himself as a Shepherd, telling Peter to feed His sheep after His resurrection. King David started out as a shepherd boy and went on to be a "man after [God's] own heart" (Acts 13:22). The royal priesthood has always been associated with taking care of God's flock. So when Peter exhorts us to be shepherds of God's flock, he is reminding us that we have been chosen to carry on the royal priesthood.

Although it is a high honor in the eyes of God, a shepherd's life is not always an easy one and tends to be lonely at times. It is a life of patience and caring. Even when you do a good job, it doesn't pay very well, and it's often thankless. Yet, if we give up our selfish desires and follow after the heart of God, we will receive a crown of glory that will never fade away. And our service to others will draw us closer to Him. Have you ever thought of yourself as a priest? Does this change your perspective on service?

56

Eyewitness Encounter: "We're Husbands, Fathers, and Servants"

Be very careful, then, how you live—not as unwise but as wise,
making the most of every opportunity, because the days are evil.
EPHESIANS 5:15–16

I clearly remember the day I brought home a new car stereo and speakers for my 1972 Nova. I was so excited to rip out all the old components and install the new ones. My dad, on the other hand, wasn't excited in the least. In fact, he was livid that I was foolish enough to make such a large purchase at the age of sixteen. Yeah, in hindsight it was pretty foolish, but it didn't seem so at the time.

Years have passed since then, and I have learned that my dad is a very wise man. Even though he was pretty upset, I now understand that what he really wanted was for me to gain some wisdom about money. He wanted me to appreciate what I had.

When it comes to being a husband, father, and servant, I know that I have to make wise choices—whether it's buying a new stereo for my car or serving my wife and children. The apostle Paul reminds us to make the most of every opportunity. Making wise choices and serving my family will open the door to more opportunities for me to be the man of God I am called to be.

—Darryl, Senior Pastor

57

Spiritual Nudge: Charles H. Spurgeon on Confidence

> *"And you, Solomon my son, know the God of your father
> and serve him with a whole heart and with a willing mind,
> for the* LORD *searches all hearts and understands every plan
> and thought. If you seek him, he will be found by you,
> but if you forsake him, he will cast you off forever."*
>
> 1 CHRONICLES 28:9 ESV

Let us go forward into the unknown future, linked eternally with Jesus. If the men of the world should cry, "Who is this that cometh up from the wilderness, leaning upon her beloved?" (Song of Solomon 8:5 KJV) we will joyfully confess that we do lean on Jesus and that we mean to lean on Him more and more. Our faithful God is an ever-flowing well of delight, and our fellowship with the Son of God is a full river of joy. Knowing these glorious things, we cannot be discouraged.[11]

---

11. Charles H. Spurgeon, *All of Grace* (Chicago: Moody, 1992), 125.

58

Bible Wisdom:
Christ on the Vine and the Branches

FROM JOHN 15:1–8

"I am the true vine, and my Father is the gardener. He cuts off every branch in me that bears no fruit, while every branch that does bear fruit he prunes so that it will be even more fruitful. You are already clean because of the word I have spoken to you. Remain in me, as I also remain in you. No branch can bear fruit by itself; it must remain in the vine. Neither can you bear fruit unless you remain in me.

"I am the vine; you are the branches. If you remain in me and I in you, you will bear much fruit; apart from me you can do nothing. If you do not remain in me, you are like a branch that is thrown away and withers; such branches are picked up, thrown into the fire and burned. If you remain in me and my words remain in you, ask whatever you wish, and it will be done for you. This is to my Father's glory, that you bear much fruit, showing yourselves to be my disciples."

59

My Prayer of Consecration and Dedication: Launching Servants

He withdrew about a stone's throw beyond them,
knelt down and prayed, "Father, if you are willing,
take this cup from Me; yet not my will, but yours be done."
LUKE 22:41–42

Jesus' prayer on the Mount of Olives is a perfect example of this type of prayer. During those tense moments before He was arrested—and ultimately led to the cross—the Lord committed Himself to God's will and asked His heavenly Father to set His course and guide His steps. We see another example of commitment to the will of the Father in Hannah's prayer of dedication. She committed Samuel to the Lord in 1 Samuel 1:24–28.

We engage in a prayer of consecration and dedication when we face two (or more) choices and don't have a clear sense about which one the Lord wants us to make. When the direction is unclear, and any of the options appear to be legitimate, righteous options, it's a good idea to get on our knees and say, "Lord, if it be Your will, I'm going to make this choice: _____. 'Yet not my will, but yours be done.'"

My Prayer of Consecration and Dedication:

_____

_____

_____

_____

_____

_____

60

My Prayers: "Lord, Not My Will, But Yours Be Done. . ."

"My teaching is not my own. It comes from the one who sent me. Anyone who chooses to do the will of God will find out whether my teaching comes from God or whether I speak on my own."
JOHN 7:16–17

God's Will for My Family:

_____
_____
_____
_____
_____
_____

God's Will for My Friends:

_____
_____
_____
_____
_____

God's Will for My Church:

_____
_____
_____
_____
_____

God's Will for My Workplace:

_____

_____

_____

_____

_____

_____

PART THREE

A Church Without Walls

61

It Begins at Home

Start children off on the way they should go,
and even when they are old they will not turn from it.
PROVERBS 22:6

Spiritual formation begins at home.

Beth—a mother of three in Colorado—points out that growing a family's faith should be every parent's *priority*. "It's a team effort," she says. "Bible teaching at church is invaluable, but spiritual training really happens at home. So my husband and I look for creative ways of engaging our children. We try to make Bible study experiential, and we involve the whole family."

Beth is right. After all, the family is the oldest and most basic of human and biblical institutions. The Bible stresses its importance as a training ground for mature adult character. The family is to be a community of teaching and learning about God and godliness. Children must be instructed and encouraged to use that instruction as a basis for their lives (Genesis 18:18, 19; Deuteronomy 4:9; 6:6–8; 11:18–21; Ephesians 6:4).

What's more, the family is meant to function as a spiritual unit. Joshua set an example when he said, "As for me and my household, we will serve the LORD" (Joshua 24:15). And get this: The Early New Testament Church was started in houses—*within families.*

Is your family growing in God—*together*? Take your spiritual temperature, and then find creative ways of having church. . .right at home!

62
Servant Family

Dear children, let us not love with words
or tongue but with actions and in truth.
1 JOHN 3:18

Instead of simply telling children to be the hands and feet of Jesus, why not take them to your local soup kitchen or rescue mission to "get their hands dirty"? Volunteer to help those less fortunate by serving them. Or consider participating with them on a summer missions trip.

My husband, Michael, and I have participated in numerous trips with churches and para-church ministries. We've rolled up our sleeves and have worked right alongside other parents and their kids—and have witnessed countless life-changing moments on the missions field.

Once your children see true poverty face-to-face—once they *experience* it—the reality crawls underneath their skin and right into their hearts. When they've seen people living in cardboard boxes, they will think twice before complaining about what Mom is making for dinner or about having to clean their room. [12]

How can your household or church become a servant family? What are some steps you can take to experience your own life-changing moments?

---

12. Michael Ross and Susie Shellenberger, *What Your Son Isn't Telling You* (Minneapolis, Minnesota: Bethany House Publishers, 2010), 37.

63

A Heritage of Love

"For who is greater, the one who is at the table or the one who serves? Is it not the one who is at the table? But I am among you as one who serves."

LUKE 22:27

If you're a parent, you work hard to give your kids a happy childhood. But you also know that each one of your children has a very distinct personality and that they process your efforts differently. One child may be ready to fight while the other tends to withdraw; one may cry easily while the other makes jokes. So what's one thing you can do for your family that everyone will appreciate? Let each child know that they are loved and accepted for who they are.

Celebrate, without labeling, the different personalities that make up your family. Make your home a safe haven for your children. They will all have a bad day from time to time. Make sure they know that they can always come home to a loving environment. Sometimes it's hard for them to see past their current situation. Often, their whole world rotates around their friends, school, and (for teens) whoever they have a crush on.

Create an environment where they are free from harassment and judgment; a place where the rules are the same for everyone. Encourage your children to support each other. Help them grasp the bigger picture. One day they will all be older, live in other places and have their own families. Help them realize that their possibilities are endless. And no matter where they go or what they do with their lives, they are loved and accepted within the family.

64

A Solid Foundation

*So he got up from the meal, took off his outer clothing, and wrapped
a towel around his waist. After that, he poured water into a
basin and began to wash his disciples' feet, drying them
with the towel that was wrapped around him.*

JOHN 13:4–5

When did God last surprise you and your loved ones?

Before Jesus allowed his followers to come to the table, he knelt before them and *cleaned them*, washing the dirt of long travels from their sore, sandal-clad feet. The disciples were shocked and amazed. Jesus took the place of the lowliest servant in the house, not the conquering king. The scriptures tell us that He did not seek worldly power to define Himself. Neither should we. Humility is a surprisingly powerful trait all on its own.

The true hierarchy of the Kingdom, "the last shall be first," forms the solid foundation for the house that God is building (Matthew 20:16 KJV). But He must build it *within us* before He can build it *through us*. The foundational work of the Spirit starts deep in our heart.

On this journey of servant leadership within our homes and our churches, the Lord will surprise us again and again. It will not always be easy, in fact at times it will be quite painful. But we must resist the temptation to grasp for power and identity apart from Christ.

Be brave and courageous as you serve the Lord with grace and humility. And expect surprises.

65

Eyewitness Encounter: "I Learned to Pray in the Kitchen"

*You shall teach them diligently to your children, and shall
talk of them when you sit in your house, when you walk
by the way, when you lie down, and when you rise up.*

DEUTERONOMY 6:7 NKJV

I am amazed how my parents continue to guide me into my adulthood. Even though I lost my father ten years ago and my mother one year ago, their impact on my life is ever present. Their voices are in my heart, and the lessons they taught me about God and life are still coming through loud and clear. Each day I am flooded with memories of all the things we would do together.

I recall the seemingly insignificant moments of cooking, gardening, walking together, and family prayers. These were the teaching moments that still instruct me and fill me with joy now. They were the moments that mattered then and now.

My mother would recite scripture and poetry, sing, and tell me stories while we cooked, gardened, and cleaned together.

My father would explain scripture to me and teach me right from wrong. I would follow him around the yard while he gardened and pepper him with questions. I loved being right where he was. He spent hours reading his Bible and could often be found in the morning on his knees praying at our living room sofa.

We prayed together as a family at that same sofa/altar. It was a place of hope and healing. These memories sustain me.

—**Nancy, Librarian**

66

Spiritual Nudge: Dr. James Dobson on Building a Spiritual Heritage

Fathers, do not embitter your children,
or they will become discouraged.

Colossians 3:21

This mission of introducing one's children to the Christian faith can be likened to a three-man relay race. . . . My most important reason for living is to get the baton—the Gospel—safely in the hands of my children. Of course, I want to place it in as many other hands as possible, and I'm deeply devoted to the ministry to families that God has given me. Nevertheless, my number one responsibility is to evangelize my own children.

In the words of my dad, everything else appears "pale and washed out" when compared with that fervent desire. Unless my son and daughter grasp the faith and take it with them around the track, it matters little how fast they run. Being first across the finish line is meaningless unless they carry the baton with them.[13]

13. Dr. James Dobson, "A Man and His Ultimate Priority," James Dobson's Family Talk, © 2014, http://drjamesdobson.org/articles/families-on-the-front-lines/a-man-and-his-ultimate-priority.

67

Bible Wisdom: Paul on Giving Generously

FROM 2 CORINTHIANS 8:1–7

And now, brothers and sisters, we want you to know about the grace that God has given the Macedonian churches. In the midst of a very severe trial, their overflowing joy and their extreme poverty welled up in rich generosity. For I testify that they gave as much as they were able, and even beyond their ability. Entirely on their own, they urgently pleaded with us for the privilege of sharing in this service to the Lord's people. And they exceeded our expectations: They gave themselves first of all to the Lord, and then by the will of God also to us. So we urged Titus, just as he had earlier made a beginning, to bring also to completion this act of grace on your part. But since you excel in everything—in faith, in speech, in knowledge, in complete earnestness and in the love we have kindled in you—see that you also excel in this grace of giving.

68

Be a Team Player

For those who serve well as deacons gain a good standing for themselves and also great confidence in the faith that is in Christ Jesus.
1 TIMOTHY 3:13 ESV

How many times do we find ourselves thinking through all the things we could have said after the discussion or moment or argument has long passed? We wish we had been bolder or more clever than we were.

So many times we know what to say, but we lack the boldness to make a difference in someone's life. We feel that gentle urging of the Lord toward approaching a stranger or an acquaintance or even a family member, but we don't think they will accept our words of encouragement. However, we must recognize that if we have "served well," we gain a "great assurance" or a "great boldness" (KJV) and can have the confidence to speak to others in any situation. As long as we speak and act with loving hearts that care for and lift up those He sends us to, then we are performing a noble task (verse 1).

So step out in faith and have confidence in the Lord. We really do need each other.

69

Real Connections

Love must be sincere. Hate what is evil; cling to what is good. Be devoted to one another in love. Honor one another above yourselves. Never be lacking in zeal, but keep your spiritual fervor, serving the Lord. Be joyful in hope, patient in affliction, faithful in prayer. Share with the Lord's people who are in need. Practice hospitality.

ROMANS 12:9–13

Some believe the Bible is an instruction manual that tells us how to be Christian. In some ways this is true. But because we have a desire to get to know Jesus—who He is, how He loves, how He thinks and feels about everything, about us—God's Word becomes quite a different book.

Instead of focusing on the rules and regulations, try looking at the Bible as a love story revolving around us. You'll find that God's laws are a reflection of what the Lord has put inside of us—His Spirit—and we can feel reassured that He is helping us love, serve, and give according to His will. Instead of a list of impossible tasks put upon a hard and disconnected heart, God's Word affirms that our hearts are connected with His and with others—hearts that are being transformed into His likeness.

Looking for a real connection? Engage the Bible—and look for Jesus in the pages of scripture.

70

The Body Needs You

And he gave the apostles, the prophets, the evangelists, the shepherds and teachers, to equip the saints for the work of ministry, for building up the body of Christ, until we all attain to the unity of the faith and of the knowledge of the Son of God, to mature manhood, to the measure of the stature of the fullness of Christ, so that we may no longer be children, tossed to and fro by the waves and carried about by every wind of doctrine, by human cunning, by craftiness in deceitful schemes.

EPHESIANS 4:11–14 ESV

The apostle Paul points out that all who know Jesus as Savior are members of one Body, united in and by the Lord. So it's time for some maturity; time for each one of us to grow deeper in our faith and take our place in God's kingdom.

"Rather, speaking the truth in love, we are to grow up in every way into him who is the head, into Christ, from whom the whole body, joined and held together by every joint with which it is equipped, when each part is working properly, makes the body grow so that it builds itself up in love" (Ephesians 4:15–16 ESV).

What gifts has God given you? What role do you play in the Body?

71

It Takes Courage

*I eagerly expect and hope that I will in no way be ashamed,
but will have sufficient courage so that now as always Christ
will be exalted in my body, whether by life or by death.
For to me, to live is Christ and to die is gain.*

PHILIPPIANS 1:20–21

He is no fool who gives what he cannot keep to gain what he cannot lose.[14]

Jim Elliot wrote these words during his youth, never imagining that he'd one day immortalize them—with his very life.

Many years later, Jim and four friends—Peter Fleming, Ed McCully, Nate Saint, and Roger Youderian—were in the middle of a lush green jungle in Ecuador. It was a deceptive place: beautiful on the surface, yet dangerous at its core. It was a land filled with deadly animals and hostile tribes—a forgotten corner of the world that these men were determined to reach with the Gospel.

It is also where they laid down their lives for the cause of Christ. In her book, *Shadow of the Almighty*, Jim's wife, Elisabeth Elliot, summed up what happened:

> *Committing themselves and all their carefully laid plans to Him
> who had so unmistakably brought them thus far, they waited for the
> Aucas. Before 4:30 that afternoon, the quiet waters of the Curaray
> flowed over the bodies of the five comrades, slain by the men they
> had come to win for Christ, whose banner they had borne. The
> world called it a nightmare of tragedy. The world did not recognize
> the truth of the second clause in Jim Elliot's credo: "He is no fool
> who gives what he cannot keep to gain what he cannot lose."[15]*

14. Elisabeth Elliot, *Shadow of the Almighty* (New York: Harper & Row, 1958), 18–19.
15. Ibid.

Our love for others is evidence of our love for God. Are you freely giving what you cannot keep?

72

Eyewitness Encounter: "We Were the Church"

"In the same way your Father in heaven is not willing that any of these little ones should perish."
MATTHEW 18:14

I was a poor college kid. I had a typical dorm room full of dirty clothes and textbooks. But I also had an unusual poster hanging on my wall. It was a large photo of a Romanian orphan. When I looked into his eyes, they cried out to me. But I was just a poor college student. What could I do? I had no idea who this child was or how I could help. I knew that others were doing great missionary work in Romania and helping the orphans. Yet God continued to call me into service every time I looked at that child. Within eight months of hanging that poster on my dorm room wall, I was in Romania. But I still didn't know much about orphans or how to help them. But I spent nine months in Romania seeking God's will. I never met the child from the poster, but I did meet so many others that needed a Savior. And they all reminded me that God was calling me to get out of my comfort zone and serve others.

In His last few moments on earth, Jesus said to *go*. That child, like so many others, just needed someone to respond to that command. If God can use a poor college student, He can certainly use you. Be the one that goes in His name.

—Kevin, Senior Pastor

Spiritual Nudge:
Darrell Guder on Worshiping "Missionally"

*"Therefore go and make disciples of all nations, baptizing them
in the name of the Father and of the Son and of the Holy Spirit."*
MATTHEW 28:19

Above all, the public worship of the mission community always leads to the pivotal act of sending. The community that is called together is the community that is sent. Every occasion of public worship is a sending event. Our worship traditions have vast resources to draw on to implement this vision of missional worship. But much work needs to be done in order to equip those who lead worship to do so with such a vision. Communities need to learn to worship missionally. This worship cannot happen merely as the result of liturgical innovation, nor will it be accomplished by converting the meeting into an evangelistic crusade meeting. Rather, the conversion of worship to its missional centeredness will come about as communities are gripped by their vocation to be Christ's witness and begin to practice that calling.[16]

16. Darrell L. Guder, *Missional Church: A Vision for the Sending of the Church in North America* (Grand Rapids, Michigan, William B. Eerdmans Publishing Company, 1998), p. 243.

74

Bible Wisdom: Paul on Being Sensitive to Others

From 1 Thessalonians 5:12–24

Now we ask you, brothers and sisters, to acknowledge those who work hard among you, who care for you in the Lord and who admonish you. Hold them in the highest regard in love because of their work. Live in peace with each other. And we urge you, brothers and sisters, warn those who are idle and disruptive, encourage the disheartened, help the weak, be patient with everyone. Make sure that nobody pays back wrong for wrong, but always strive to do what is good for each other and for everyone else.

Rejoice always, pray continually, give thanks in all circumstances; for this is God's will for you in Christ Jesus.

Do not quench the Spirit. Do not treat prophesies with contempt but test them all; hold on to what is good, reject every kind of evil.

May God himself, the God of peace, sanctify you through and through. May your whole spirit, soul and body be kept blameless at the coming of our Lord Jesus Christ. The one who calls you is faithful, and he will do it.

75

Who Is Your Neighbor?

Let brotherly love continue. Do not neglect to show hospitality
to strangers, for thereby some have entertained angels unawares.
Remember those who are in prison, as though in prison with them,
and those who are mistreated, since you also are in the body.
HEBREWS 13:1–3 ESV

The word *remember* appears in the scriptures more than two hundred times. Throughout Hebrews 13, it is used as an encouragement to keep in our minds at all times those who have gone before us.

We almost have to tie a string around our finger for this message, because it's easy at times to get caught up in what we are doing and forget to see the bigger picture—that we stand on the shoulders of those who have gone before and we are building on the foundations they have laid. When we stand together with them one day in glory, we will thank them for keeping us in mind, the brothers and sisters who would come after them, and for paving the way for us.

We, in turn, should work to reach out and bring other brothers and sisters into the kingdom of God so they can join us on that glorious day.

So who is your neighbor? Who has gone before you? Take a moment to remember them.

76

Open Your Eyes

*Trust in the LORD with all your heart and lean not on
your own understanding. In all your ways submit to him,
and he will make your paths straight.*

PROVERBS 3:5–6

I used to have one of those posters comprised of different colored dots.
And if you stared at it long enough, in just the right way, you would
suddenly see a picture of a dolphin. Do you remember those? For a while,
these types of posters and books were everywhere. But several of my
friends could never see the picture. They tried everything, but it never
came into focus for them.

Sometimes I feel the same way about God's mission. We seek,
study, and try all the different "tricks," but it just doesn't come into focus.
Is it impossible for some to see it clearly? We are all blinded by our
brokenness, which makes it difficult to see beyond our own filters. But
the amazing thing about God's mission is simply that it is God's. He
is the author of the story, and He will open our eyes to it when He
knows we're ready. We could never see it on our own. But if we open
ourselves up to the Spirit, He will lead us where we need to go. He will
open the doors, give us peace, and amaze us with His timing. So don't
worry about if you are serving Him in the right position. If you are
seeking His will, He will place you in the right place at the right time.

Do you feel lost about where to serve? Have you really opened
yourself up to the Spirit for direction and guidance?

77

You're the One He's Sending

"The King will reply, 'Truly I tell you, whatever you did for one of the least of these brothers and sisters of mine, you did for me.'"
MATTHEW 25:40

I once had a really great boss. He made us work very hard, but he also took care of us. If we had to work late, he brought us dinner. If we were being mistreated by others, he would step in and dissolve the situation. He pushed us hard, but also rewarded our good work. He was open to new ideas and suggestions, too. But I soon learned that if I made a good suggestion, it would then become my responsibility. I once asked why we didn't recycle. Within a week I was the recycling coordinator. One time I complained that the snow had not been cleared from the sidewalk. I spent the next two hours shoveling snow. These weren't punishments, they were training. He was trying to teach me that we are given insights so we can do something about them.

God works the same way. He gives us eyes to see the needs of others so we can act on fulfilling those needs. He imparts His creativity so we can discover new ways of operating. He breaks our heart for those in pain so we can be there for them. Sometimes, this is how He pulls us into His mission.

Do you recognize a need that isn't being met? Is it possible that God wants you to act on that insight?

78

Start as Friends

And let us consider one another in
order to stir up love and good works.
HEBREWS 10:24 NKJV

Instead of treating nonbelievers as a project, start as friends. "'Love the Lord your God with all your heart and with all your soul and with all your mind.' This is the first and greatest commandment. And the second is like it: 'Love your neighbor as yourself'" (Matthew 22:37–39).

And to be effective witnesses, Christ-followers must. . .

Know what we believe (and why) by engaging the Bible daily. (We can't share with others what we don't know.)

Believe what we know by trusting Jesus Christ daily. (We can't convince others of something we doubt.)

Live what we know and consistently "practice what we preach." (We can't say one thing, then live another way.)

Ready to "stir up love and good works"? Share the Gospel with a friend.

79

Eyewitness Encounter:
"I Love My City"

Each of you should use whatever gift you have received to serve others, as faithful stewards of God's grace in its various forms.

1 PETER 4:10

A decade ago I said a prayer that completely altered my life. My kids had just been diagnosed with a rare genetic condition that would affect all of our lives. In a few years they'd be wheelchair-bound. I left my job in corporate America to be with the kids. Four months later, my pastor had hired me to be a part-time youth and family minister. I'd been a Christian for years at this point, but I felt God asking for even more.

So I prayed: "Father God, what more do you want from me? I'm a mess. I don't even know how to deal with my situation. But I know you want more. Open my eyes. Help me to see people as you see them, to really see them. Help me to love them as you love them. In Jesus' name. Amen."

And He did. He opened my eyes and my heart. I didn't know how or where the journey would take me, but I knew change was underway. Ten years later, I'm now part of an exciting new church. I never expected one prayer to change my life so much. The journey hasn't always been easy, but I will remain faithful because I know that God loves me and helps me to love my city.

—**Anne, Pastor**

80

Spiritual Nudge: Lester DeKoster on "Thread to Fabric"

*And let us consider how we may spur
one another on toward love and good deeds.*

HEBREWS 10:24

If we put a painting under a microscope, it becomes apparent that each color exists thanks to innumerable tiny dots. If we analyze a television screen, it is evident that the figures we see are in fact visible because each is composed of small individual units. And if we could trace our automobiles back through all the steps involved in make them, we would find workers' hands investing workers' selves every step of the way. All wholes are made up of individual parts. What matters, always, is not who can count the parts or how readily each part *could* have been replaced. What matters is that the job, each job, like yours or mine, has a doer and gets done.

Unless many workers just like ourselves did give themselves to making the chairs we are now sitting on, we would be sitting on the floor. Unless, of course, nobody ever invested himself in making the floor. Then we would be sitting on the grass out in the backyard—unless nobody ever planted and mowed the grass! In a world without work being done by countless and anonymous someones, we would all be Tarzans swinging from tree to tree.

The day we went to work, we locked hands with humankind in weaving the texture of civilized life—and our lives each found the key to meaning.

Our thread counts because it is *done*![17]

---

17. Lester DeKoster, *Work: The Meaning of Your Life* (Grand Rapids, Michigan, Christian's Library Press, 1982), p. 42.

81

Bible Wisdom: Christ on Loving Your Neighbor

FROM MATTHEW 22:37–40

" 'Love the Lord your God with all your heart and with all your soul and with all your mind.' This is the first and greatest commandment. And the second is like it: 'Love your neighbor as yourself.' All the Law and the Prophets hang on these two commandments."

82

God's Church around the World

For God did not send his Son into the world to condemn the world,
but to save the world through him. Whoever believes in him is not
condemned, but whoever does not believe stands condemned already
because they have not believed in the name of God's one and only Son.
JOHN 3:17–18

I can remember so many sermons when the preacher would say, "Don't worry, God probably won't send you to Africa; He wants you to serve Him right here and right now." And this is true most of the time. But I was the strange little child that secretly wished that God would send me to Africa. I wanted to explore strange new places and learn how other people lived. I loved to meet missionaries and hear their stories. I've always been happy that God wants to reach the whole world. Maybe I would get to be the one He sends.

I signed up for a summer of missionary work when I was in college. I was so excited about the idea that I would end up in South America, Africa, or any other country. So I was very disappointed when I received my assignment to go to Connecticut. That's right. I was going all the way to New England. But once I got there, I was overwhelmed by the people in need and how they were searching for God. The summer was very demanding, and we reached a lot of people. And I learned that God really does need us to go into all the world—even if it's just down the road. Are you willing to go wherever He leads? Even if it doesn't fit your own desires or expectations?

83

Why Not?

Still another said, "I will follow you, Lord; but first let me go back and say goodbye to my family." Jesus replied, "No one who puts a hand to the plow and looks back is fit for service in the kingdom of God."

LUKE 9:61–62

I am the queen of excuses: I'm tired. I'm bored. I'm too busy. I'll get to that later. Nobody told me. I misunderstood. And so on. This list could continue indefinitely. And these are all legitimate reasons why some things just don't get done in my life. But occasionally I must step back and reevaluate my priorities. When I'm too busy to spend time with my family, I'm too busy. When I go days or weeks without reading by Bible, I'm too busy. When I'm too overextended and forget to take care of those around me, I'm too busy.

We only have twenty-four hours in a day. And we only have a limited amount of days here on earth. I'm fearful that I will spend most of them running from place to place, getting errands done. I know they need to be done, but not at the expense of my time with God, or my family, or my church. God has set our priorities for us. He has called us to put Him first. And then love all others as we love ourselves. I'm not sure that picking up the dry cleaning or mowing the lawn would remain very high on our list if we compared it to His list. Are your priorities in the correct order? Are we placing other things before God and His mission?

84

See the Bigger Picture

"I am sending you out like sheep among wolves.
Therefore be as shrewd as snakes and as innocent as doves."
MATTHEW 10:16

Serving the Lord can be challenging. God has not called us to stay safely tucked away, surrounded by like-minded people. Yes, we are to be active members of our faith communities, but He is also sending us *out* to the world. The same world where we live, work, shop, vacation, and relax is where we are to serve others and love them with the love of God. But if we don't understand what we are getting into, we won't last long. Humbly loving others can be brutal. Sometimes we will be accepted and loved, but most of the time we will be misunderstood and ridiculed. That is why He was warned us to be prepared for the battle. We are to be smart as we live a life of pure devotion to Him and His ways. We are to be so connected to Him that the Spirit can lead our steps.

Understanding the Lord's larger mission helps us move forward when the situation right in front of us seems too overwhelming. Our hope is in Him, and the promise of our future helps us avoid distractions. Let's press on as God opens our eyes to His mission.

Do you see the larger picture? Do you know you have a place in His mission?

85

The Whole World Is in His Hands

"For there will never cease to be poor in the land. Therefore I command you, 'You shall open wide your hand to your brother, to the needy and to the poor, in your land.'"

DEUTERONOMY 15:11 ESV

How open-handed the Lord is with us!

We may not be as rich financially as we want, and sometimes the good things of this world may elude us, but we have an open-handed, gracious Father who loves us and will give us all things in their season. Just as He gave us Himself, His only Son, and His sweet Holy Spirit, He remains faithful and true, loving us in any circumstance every second of every day.

This is why He calls us to be generous as well—to show the world who He is. Jesus pointed out that the woman who gave only two mites gave the most. When we give to others, not just money but also grace and forgiveness and gentle words, He is with us, and His love can shine through us.

We have no need to fear or worry. He has the whole world in His open hands and will never tighten His fist and crush us. Instead He will always hold us faithfully, gently, tenderly in His strong, powerful hands.

Do you trust that He has the whole world in His hands? Remember—nothing goes unnoticed or unrewarded by the One who loves His creation enough to die for it.

86

Eyewitness Encounter: "The Summer that Changed My Life"

Command those who are rich in this present world not to be arrogant nor to put their hope in wealth, which is so uncertain, but to put their hope in God, who richly provides us with everything for our enjoyment.

1 TIMOTHY 6:17

What fourteen-year-old doesn't dream big? I was constantly thinking about the future—who I'd marry, where I'd live, what I wanted to do with my life. Becoming the next Nolan Ryan was a pretty high priority at the time.

Never could I have imagined what the future held on all three counts. I have an extraordinary wife, who has joined me for several years in Europe as a volunteer missionary. As a visiting instructor in church history and theology, I've met many people with amazing stories who are training to become pastors in challenging societies. These people and experiences have changed my life far more than any way I might have contributed to theirs.

It all started, though, in a kind of "blink-and-you'll-miss-it" moment. My youth pastor pulled me aside on a Wednesday night and said someone I knew anonymously gave me seven hundred dollars toward my upcoming mission trip to Mexico. It was amazing. I would have never been able to raise that kind of money myself. I didn't think I was going to get to go. But thanks to that individual, whose name I've never learned, my life was sent quietly spinning in a whole new direction because of their generosity.

My dreams of throwing 100 mph fastballs are long over. But that summer in Mexico was a major step that led to a life of wonder, transformation, and adventure far beyond even my considerable imagination.

—Andrew, Doctoral Student

87

Spiritual Nudge: David Livingstone on Serving the World

"Therefore go and make disciples of all nations, baptizing them in the name of the Father and of the Son and of the Holy Spirit."

MATTHEW 28:19

"Go!" This single command defined Dr. David Livingstone's life.

Stay at home? Sit quietly in the safety of Scotland? Pursue a life of wealth and comfort? For this young doctor-turned-missionary, these weren't even options worth considering.

"Whatever way my life may be spent as best to promote the glory of our gracious God, I feel anxious to do it," he told a friend as he set off to Africa's vast Kalahari wilderness.[20]

It was the summer of 1841, and stretched out before him were endless savannahs, mysterious tribes, unsaved souls—and a God-sized assignment.

Dr. Livingstone never doubted his call to "take an eternal risk in Africa." The way he saw it, the Gospel itself was the account of Jesus leaving His Father's right hand to go to Calvary. Likewise, Christ instructs those who want to be His disciples to leave their comforts and follow Him.

In a letter to his sister, Janet, Dr. Livingstone wrote:

Let us seek—and with the conviction that we cannot do without it—that all selfishness be extirpated, pride banished, unbelief driven from the mind, every idol dethroned, and everything hostile to holiness and opposed to the divine will be crucified; that "holiness to the Lord" may be engraven on the heart, and evermore characterize our whole conduct.[18]

18. J. H. Worcester, Jr., *The Life of David Livingstone* (Chicago: Moody, n.d.), 14.

Sam Wellman, *David Livingstone—Missionary and Explorer* (Uhrichsville, Ohio: Barbour, n.d.), 41.

88

Bible Wisdom: John on Celebration

FROM REVELATION 19:1–9 MSG

I heard a sound like massed choirs in Heaven singing,
Hallelujah!
The salvation and glory and power are God's—
his judgments true, his judgments just.
He judged the great Whore
who corrupted the earth with her lust.
He avenged on her the blood of his servants.
Then, more singing:
Hallelujah!
The smoke from her burning billows up
to high Heaven forever and ever and ever.
The Twenty-four Elders and the Four Animals fell to their
knees and worshiped God on his Throne, praising,
Amen! Yes! Hallelujah!
From the Throne came a shout, a command:
Praise our God, all you his servants,
All you who fear him, small and great!
Then I heard the sound of massed choirs, the sound of a mighty
cataract, the sound of strong thunder:
Hallelujah!
The Master reigns,
our God, the Sovereign-Strong!
Let us celebrate, let us rejoice,
let us give him the glory!
The Marriage of the Lamb has come;
his Wife has made herself ready.
She was given a bridal gown

of bright and shining linen.

The linen is the righteousness of the saints.

The Angel said to me, "Write this: 'Blessed are those invited to the Wedding Supper of the Lamb.'" He added, "These are the true words of God!"

89

My Prayer of Praise and Worship: Glorifying God

The shepherds returned, glorifying and praising God for all the things they had heard and seen, which were just as they had been told.

LUKE 2:20

These types of prayers express our love and adoration for the Lord. In them, we praise God and thank Him for His mercy and many blessings in our lives, and we tell Him how much we love Him. It's not uncommon for prayers of praise and worship to involve shouting, singing, clapping, crying, laughing, jumping, dancing. . .and other outbursts of joyful emotion!

The Bible is filled with many examples. Here are a few highlights:

Luke 11:2: In the Lord's Prayer, Jesus instructs his disciples to praise God: "When you pray, say: 'Our Father in heaven, hallowed be Your name.'"

Luke 18:43: The blind man who was healed by Jesus is described as "glorifying God." And all the people who witnessed the miracle "gave praise to God." They prayed prayers of thanksgiving.

John 11:41: As Jesus stands outside the tomb of Lazarus, moments before he raises his friend from the dead, the Lord looks up and says, "Father, I thank You that You have heard Me."

My Prayer of Praise and Worship:

_____

_____

_____

_____

_____

90

My Prayers: "Lord, We Praise and Worship You. . ."

Shout for joy to the Lord, all the earth. Worship the Lord with gladness; come before him with joyful songs. Know that the Lord is God. It is he who made us, and we are his; we are his people, the sheep of his pasture. Enter his gates with thanksgiving and his courts with praise; give thanks to him and praise his name. For the Lord is good and his love endures forever; his faithfulness continues through all generations.

PSALM 100:1–5

Praises for My Family:

_____
_____
_____
_____
_____
_____

Praises for My Friends:

_____
_____
_____
_____
_____
_____

Praises for My Church:

_____
_____
_____
_____
_____
_____
_____

Praises for My Workplace:

_____
_____
_____
_____
_____
_____

PART FOUR

Prepare for the Mission

91

Start Your Day with Prayer

Very early in the morning, while it was still dark, Jesus got up, left the house and went off to a solitary place, where he prayed.

MARK 1:35

So often we come to the Lord in prayer when we find ourselves in a tight spot or need some guidance. Coming before Him is like tapping into a lifeline. Praise, confession, and petition are important in our lives. Spending time with God helps us recognize that it is His mission we are on. He is the one who sets the goals and leads us through our days. Beginning our day with prayer helps us to start each day with the correct mind set. It helps us focus on Him instead of our to-do lists. It reminds us why we dedicate so much time to others. In prayer we find the inner peace and strength to face each day. Let Him be your encourager. Let Him carry you through. He desires to be the one who sustains you as you serve Him. It's how He works. How did you begin your day today?

92

An Honest Conversation with God

Therefore confess your sins to each other and pray for each other so that you may be healed. The prayer of a righteous person is powerful and effective.

JAMES 5:16

There is no need to sugarcoat it. We spend too much time trying to impress other people through fake smiles, canned answers, and polite words. Unfortunately, we often try to interact with God in the same way. We try to make our prayers sound holy and proper. We answer our own questions before we've listened to what He has to say. We apologize for our emotions. And the whole time God is waiting for us to stop putting on airs and just be honest with Him. He already knows our hearts anyway. We must realize that humbling ourselves before the Lord is the only safe place in the world. Sure, there are times of correction. But we must trust that He is always working in our favor. We can get to where He is leading us so much quicker if we just come before Him honestly and reverently. He can handle the truth. Remember, He is the source of all truth. And it is His truth that you carry to those around you. All service to others must begin with a genuine heart filled with His love.

93

Prayer: Personal and Public

Therefore I want the men everywhere to pray,
lifting up holy hands without anger or disputing.
1 TIMOTHY 2:8

Prayer is a very personal matter. It is a direct connection with God Himself. For this reason, so many people prefer to keep their prayers private. We are even instructed in scripture not to parade around praying in public to make ourselves look good, because that's not prayer at all—it's self-promotion. But there is a time for public prayer. There are very special moments when God's people join together as one in times of praise and petition. Sometimes this takes place on Sunday morning. Other times it may take place in a small group meeting or in Sunday school. Other times, we must set an example as individuals when we teach children and adults how to pray. This is acceptable and pleasing to God as long as our prayers are sincere and honest. So be encouraged to stay connected to God through prayer, both privately and publicly.

94

Hearing from God

"But when he, the Spirit of truth, comes, he will guide you into all the truth. He will not speak on his own; he will speak only what he hears, and he will tell you what is yet to come."

JOHN 16:13

Prayer is a two-way street. We are often very good at sending our prayers to God. But we struggle when it comes to hearing from God. Why is that? It's possible that we don't slow down enough to listen. Maybe we don't want to know what God has to tell us. But most of the time, I believe we engage in prayer with a flawed understanding of what it is. Prayer is not just a time to ask for things. And it's not just a time to recognize Him as Creator and Savior. Prayer is a special gift that allows us to connect one-on-one with God. A big part of our relationship with Him is a mutual desire for connection.

So take time to silence yourself before God with a sincere heart. Take the time to push out all the outside voices, thoughts, and agendas as you seek the Lord in prayer. It will take some practice, but this is one discipline that will change your life. Have you heard from Him lately? Is He able to guide your life through prayer?

Eyewitness Encounter: "The Silent Prayer Warriors"

*But when you pray, go into your room, close the door and
pray to your Father, who is unseen. Then your Father,
who sees what is done in secret, will reward you.*

MATTHEW 6:6

Early one Saturday morning I stopped by the church to drop off a box of supplies. To my surprise, there were cars in the parking lot and the lights were on inside. I was very intrigued as I entered. At first I didn't see or hear anyone. Then I noticed an elderly gentleman at the end of the Sunday school hall. He was slowly walking in and out of every classroom. Then I saw a couple of ladies praying at the alter in the sanctuary. I dropped my box at the office and then decided to investigate a little more. I just had to know what was going on. Suddenly, a familiar face came around the corner and greeted me with a smile. I asked why people were at the church so early in the morning. He explained that for over thirty years this group of friends had been coming to the church to pray for each Sunday service, Sunday school class, and ministry of the church. They split up and walked around the church, laying hands on the chairs, tables, Bibles, whiteboards, etc., praying that we would use the tools God had given us help people grow in Christ. They specifically prayed for our church members and all of those who we haven't met yet. I suddenly knew why our church had remained solid for so many years.

—**Tiffany, Children's Pastor**

96

Spiritual Nudge: Teresa of Avila on Prayer

This is a trustworthy saying. And I want you to stress these things, so that those who have trusted in God may be careful to devote themselves to doing what is good. These things are excellent and profitable for everyone.

TITUS 3:8

Let us, therefore, place our trust in God and not in ourselves, relying heavily on his mercy and not fighting the battle alone. When you feel the beginnings of temptation, do not fight back with strenuous efforts, but rather, gently begin a time of prayer and recollection. At first it will be difficult, but after a while you will be able to do it easily, and for long periods of time.

Do not think about that you must stop doing your work in order to pray. The Lord will turn all of our work time into profit as long as we continue in a spirit of prayer. There is no remedy for the temptations that we face except to start at the beginning, and the beginning is prayer. The only way to lose is to turn back.[19]

---

19. Teresa of Avila, *The Interior Castle* (New York, New York, Paulist, 1979).

Bible Wisdom:
Nehemiah on the Faith to Rebuild

FROM NEHEMIAH 1:5–11

Then I said:

"LORD, the God of heaven, the great and awesome God, who keeps his covenant of love with those who love him and keep his commandments, let your ear be attentive and your eyes open to hear the prayer your servant is praying before you day and night for your servants, the people of Israel. I confess the sins we Israelites, including myself and my father's family, have committed against you. We have acted very wickedly toward you. We have not obeyed the commands, decrees and laws you gave your servant Moses.

"Remember the instruction you gave your servant Moses, saying, 'If you are unfaithful, I will scatter you among the nations, but if you return to me and obey my commands, then even if your exiled people are at the farthest horizon, I will gather them from there and bring them to the place I have chosen as a dwelling for my Name.'

"They are your servants and your people, whom you redeemed by your great strength and your mighty hand. Lord, let your ear be attentive to the prayer of this your servant and to the prayer of your servants who delight in revering your name. Give your servant success today by granting him favor in the presence of this man."

I was cupbearer to the king.

98

The Gift of His Word

All Scripture is God-breathed and is useful for teaching,
rebuking, correcting and training in righteousness.
2 TIMOTHY 3:16

My father was a very social person. He was constantly networking for some worthy cause in our small community. I would often tag along as he visited people in their homes for one reason or another. But there was one thing I began to notice. Almost every home had a family Bible. Sometimes they were old and well used. Other times they were sitting on a shelf covered in dust. There were a few older folks who used their Bible as a memory book. They would keep important documents or special photos tucked between the pages. But I often wondered if anyone really read these Bibles? Why was it a comfort just to have it there, sitting on a shelf like a safety net? As an adult, I have spent many hours studying this fascinating tool that God has given us. And every time I open its pages, I am amazed how the Spirit uses it to guide my life. Sometimes it offers encouragement. Other times it offers direction. And there have also been times it offers correction. I am thankful that we have been given this tool. Without it, how would we know our history? How would we connect and learn from our brothers and sisters who have gone before us? Life sure would be harder without the Bible. When is the last time you opened the pages of the Bible and asked the Spirit to speak to you?

99

The History of God's People

In the beginning was the Word, and the Word
was with God, and the Word was God.
JOHN 1:1

What is your favorite Bible story? Is it the one about how God created the earth? Maybe it's the one about the flood or the parting of the Red Sea. Don't you love the one about how Jesus was born in a manger? I can only imagine what it would have been like to watch Him ascend into heaven.

The Bible is an amazing collection of sixty-six books that contain the stories of God and His creation. And within those pages, we find a God that is beyond our wildest imagination. And yet, He continues to be a God who loves His people and offers redemption and reconciliation. We are a part of this story. We are a continuation of His work on earth. Our history can be found in the scriptures. We have a rich family history to learn from. And our hope is found in the God who is inviting us into His story. We have been adopted into an eternal family by the Father Himself. Have you ever read the scriptures like it's a family history? Have you ever realized that you are part of a long legacy of people who are all connected by God?

100
The Living Bible

For the word of God is alive and active. Sharper than any double-edged sword, it penetrates even to dividing soul and spirit, joints and marrow; it judges the thoughts and attitudes of the heart.

HEBREWS 4:12

One of the most popular Bible translations in the 1970s was called *The Living Bible*. I remember the one in our house. It had a worn-out green leather cover, and it was everyone's favorite. But as a kid, I never really understood what was *alive* about it. Even though the Bible was important, it was just words on a page to me. But later in life I began to see the brilliance in this amazing tool that God has given us. I began to experience how He uses the scriptures in the lives of His people. I could read the same passage at two different points in my life and catch a new message or nuance each time. And the message was exactly what He was trying to communicate to me, providing a new and deeper understanding of God and myself. This was the original intent of the Bible. It was designed by God to help us see the bigger picture. It offers instruction for daily and long-term living. Do you read the scriptures with expectation? Does His Word live in your heart?

101
Hide It in Our Hearts

Consequently, faith comes from hearing the message,
and the message is heard through the word about Christ.
ROMANS 10:17

I remember listening to a missionary from Africa when I was young. He told spectacular stories about life halfway around the world and the people he had met. He told of miracles and celebrations. He described what it was like to live without electricity or telephones. It was very fascinating. But I remember most vividly his stories of the hardships that Christians faced in other countries. There were stories of persecution and discrimination. He told one story about a family that lost everything because the police had found a Bible hidden under their bed. Before this, I had never thought about not having a Bible to read. I tried to imagine what it would be like to not have one. Would I remember all the stories? Had I even taken the time to read the whole thing? Did I know it well enough to remember its message if I wasn't able to pick it up and read it? This helped me realize how important it was to bring the scriptures into my heart and mind. Once I began to embrace the Bible with this type of reverence, I noticed that God began to use its words in my life. I wasn't just memorizing verses; I was opening myself up to the work of the Holy Spirit. Do you have God's story imprinted on your heart? Have you experienced how the Spirit uses it to shape your thoughts and faith as we serve others? Have you helped others, especially children, engage the Bible in ways that will last a lifetime?

102

Eyewitness Encounter: "God's Tool Kit"

*Jesus answered, "It is written: 'Man shall not live on bread alone,
but on every word that comes from the mouth of God.'"*
MATTHEW 4:4

I love bread—any kind of bread. I like it hot, cold, buttered, crunchy, with or without extra ingredients, or day old. I love the smell of bread coming out of the oven. I love to mash up the middle, making it extra thick before eating it. I guess you could say I have a bread problem. But I am also fascinated by bread. It seems to be so simple, yet it takes skill to execute properly. I remember watching my grandmother make biscuits. She would mix just the right amount of flour, baking soda, salt, and water into a large bowl and mix it with her hands. Then she would place a huge clump of dough onto a greased pan and slide it into a hot oven. Soon, the smell would fill the room and my mouth would begin to water. And approximately thirty minutes later, I would get to enjoy fresh homemade biscuits.

So I get excited when I read that we are not to live on bread alone. I know Christ is using bread as an example. And He is telling us that the wonderful kingdom He has made for us is beyond our wildest dreams. He wants us to feast on His goodness. Even the things we love the most, like bread, don't even begin to compare to its greatness. He uses all of His tools as He places the ingredients together in His perfect timing and perfectly shapes our future.

—**Gina, Grateful Granddaughter**

103

Spiritual Nudge: Madame Guyon on "Praying the Scripture"

[Jacob] had a dream in which he saw a stairway resting on the earth, with its top reaching to heaven, and the angels of God were ascending and descending on it. There above it stood the LORD, and he said: "I am the LORD, the God of your father Abraham and the God of Isaac. I will give you and your descendants the land on which you are lying. Your descendants will be like the dust of the earth, and you will spread out to the west and to the east, to the north and to the south. All peoples on earth will be blessed through you and your offspring. I am with you and will watch over you wherever you go, and I will bring you back to this land. I will not leave you until I have done what I have promised you." When Jacob awoke from his sleep, he thought, "Surely the LORD is in this place, and I was not aware of it." He was afraid and said, "How awesome is this place! This is none other than the house of God; this is the gate of heaven."

GENESIS 28:12–17

"Praying the scripture" is a unique way of dealing with the scripture; it involves both reading and prayer. Turn to the scripture; choose some passage that is simple and fairly practical. Next, come to the Lord. Come quietly and humbly. There, before him, read a small portion of the passage of scripture you have opened to.

Be careful as you read. Take in fully, gently, and carefully what you are reading. Taste it and digest it as you read. In the past it may have been your habit, while reading, to move very quickly from one verse of scripture to another until you have read the whole passage. Perhaps you were seeking to find the main point of the passage.

But in coming to the Lord by means of "praying the scripture," you do not read quickly; you read very slowly. You do not move from one passage to another, not until you have *sensed* the very heart of what you have read. You may then want to take that portion of scripture that has touched you and turn it into prayer.

After you have sensed something of the passage, and after you know that the essence of that portion has been extracted and all the deeper sense of it is gone, then, very slowly, gently, and in a calm manner begin to read the next portion of that passage. You will be surprised to find that when your time with the Lord has ended, you will have read very little, probably no more than half a page.[20]

104

Bible Wisdom: Nehemiah on Helping the Poor

FROM NEHEMIAH 5:6–13

When I heard their outcry and these charges, I was very angry. I pondered them in my mind and then accused the nobles and officials. I told them, "You are charging your own people interest!" So I called together a large meeting to deal with them and said: "As far as possible, we have bought back our fellow Jews who were sold to the Gentiles. Now you are selling your own people, only for them to be sold back to us!" They kept quiet, because they could find nothing to say.

So I continued, "What you are doing is not right. Shouldn't you walk in the fear of our God to avoid the reproach of our Gentile enemies? I and my brothers and my men are also lending the people money and grain. But let us stop charging interest! Give back to them

20. Jeanne Guyon, *Experiencing the Depths of Jesus Christ*, Edited by Gene Edwards (Goleta, California, Christian Books, 1975).

immediately their fields, vineyards, olive groves and houses, and also the interest you are charging them—one percent of the money, grain, new wine and olive oil."

"We will give it back," they said. "And we will not demand anything more from them. We will do as you say."

Then I summoned the priests and made the nobles and officials take an oath to do what they had promised. I also shook out the folds of my robe and said, "In this way may God shake out of their house and possessions anyone who does not keep this promise. So may such a person be shaken out and emptied!"

At this the whole assembly said, "Amen," and praised the LORD. And the people did as they had promised.

105

Build Your Base

So this is what the Sovereign LORD says: "See, I lay a stone in Zion,
a tested stone, a precious cornerstone for a sure foundation;
the one who relies on it will never be stricken with panic."
ISAIAH 28:16

One of the most beautiful places on earth is Great Sand Dunes National Park in Colorado. There are huge mountains in the southwest corner of Colorado. On one side there is the San Louis Valley that stretches for miles. And the Rocky Mountains loom over the dunes on the other. It's the perfect spot to reconnect with nature and try to count the endless stars in the night sky. But one of the most challenging things to try is hiking up the sand dunes. They are huge, and it seemed like every time I took one step, I'd slide three steps down. It's one of the most exhausting workouts for your calf muscles—like hiking in quicksand. There's just no way to get a strong foothold when you're standing on tons of sand.

Sometimes, this is how ministry feels. You work and work and work some more and just seem to get further behind. That is why it is so important to build your base. Be sure to spend time alone with God. Spend time with your family. Invest in solid friendships. And recruit others into your area of service. These are the ways to build a solid base that will provide firm footing when you are trying to climb a mountain of sand. Have you identified the people in your life that you can count on? Have you let them know how much you appreciate them today?

106
Seek Advice

The fear of the LORD is the beginning of knowledge,
but fools despise wisdom and instruction.
PROVERBS 1:7

I once took a class where we worked through several different case studies each week. The instructor would assign the case number, and we each had to write a response. But I didn't have the background information I needed. Instead of asking for help, I bluffed my way through the assignment. All seemed to go well until I realized that the next assignment was based on the same case. So again, I had to bluff my way through. By the third week of class, I came to understand that all of the assignments were going to be based off the information that I was missing. But it was too late to ask for help. If I did, the instructor would know that I had bluffed my first two papers. So I continued to try to guess and take chances. Finally, I couldn't fake it anymore. So I had to ask a classmate for the information. It was embarrassing, but I had to do it. It would have been so much better if I had just asked for it earlier. It would have saved me so much stress and extra work. The biggest thing I learned in that class was to ask for help when I needed it. I needed help even though I thought I could make it on my own. Are you trying to bluff your way through an assignment in life? Have you asked for advice?

107
Learning from Each Other

For everyone has heard about your obedience,
so I rejoice because of you; but I want you to be wise
about what is good, and innocent about what is evil.

ROMANS 16:19

Our pastor had announced that there was interest in redesigning the church basement. He invited anyone who could make it to show up Saturday morning for a brainstorming meeting.

At the meeting, I looked around the room and saw an interesting collection of folks. Some were older, some were younger, and some looked half-asleep. But as the pastor kicked off the brainstorming session, people perked up and really got into offering ideas for the redesign. As most meetings go, some ideas were crazy. But others made a lot of sense. At several points, people would shake their heads in agreement and say things like, "Oh, I never thought of that." In the end, we had come up with a plan, and most people had volunteered to oversee certain portions of the operation.

As we began the work, I jumped from group to group, offering help. I learned how to properly tape off widows before painting. I discovered that it is important to stain wood with the grain. I wasn't allowed near the woodworking area without safety glasses. And I was often reminded how important it was to keep a positive attitude. In the end, our church basement looked great, and most importantly, I learned not to underestimate a group of volunteers who were ready to serve God's church. Have you been surprised by anyone lately? Have you discovered the brilliance of God's plan to give us all different talents?

108

We Are Not Alone

And let us consider how we may spur one another on toward love and good deeds, not giving up meeting together, as some are in the habit of doing, but encouraging one another— and all the more as you see the Day approaching.

Hebrews 10:24–25

I grew up in a small country town. One summer it rained for several days in a row. The river rose and soon most of our town was under water. As the water flowed, families were forced out of their homes and into the living rooms and guest rooms of their neighbors on higher ground. Without power, we all anxiously watched the water rise. Then we got the word that the dam had broken and the whole town would soon be under water. So we jumped into our vehicles and headed to even higher ground. Several hundred people crammed into the little brick church building that sat on a hill above town. It was a long night of waiting and worry. People shared food and blankets. Adults played with the kids to keep them calm. The medical personal made their rounds to make sure we were all safe. And the local pastors gathered together, inviting all people to join them in prayer for the safety of everyone. It didn't matter which church you went to or in which part of town you lived. On that night, we all came together as one in a time of crisis. Thankfully, as the sun rose, we discovered that the damage wasn't as bad as we had expected. Have you experienced this type of community? It doesn't take a crisis to care for others. Are there people in your life that need a helping hand (or just a genuine smile) today?

109

Eyewitness Encounter: "Focus in the Storm"

Two are better than one, because they have a good return for their labor.
ECCLESIASTES 4:9

On the first day of our daughter's first real job, she had the following conversation:

Coworker: *"So, you're new here? Your first day?"*

Our daughter: *"Yes! Starting now!"*

Coworker: *"Welcome to hell!"*

It was not the conversation I wanted my daughter to have on her first day of work at her first "real job!" And yet, it happened. But I hardly think working as a bagger at a grocery store even comes close to hell.

In the book of Ecclesiastes, the Hebrew word that sounds like "hell" is actually *hevel*, and it is translated as "meaningless" or "futility." We could say that the Book of Ecclesiastes teaches that "life is *hevel*!"

Sometimes, ministry doesn't work out the way we expect it to. And at times, things can go completely wrong. But even on our worst days, things are not meaningless. No, we have placed our hope in the sovereign Lord of the universe who implores us to "Work hard at whatever [we] do" (Ecclesiastes 9:10 CEV). He wants us to have zeal and passion about our mission. Because it is His mission.

When life feels like hell, remember, it's not hell, but *hevel*—a fleeting time on earth to serve the One who is the Breath of all life.

—Marty, Professor

110

Spiritual Nudge: Jeremy Taylor on Focusing on Strengths

"For all those who exalt themselves will be humbled, and those who humble themselves will be exalted."

LUKE 14:11

The truly humble person will not only look admirably at the strengths of others but will also look with great forgiveness upon the weaknesses of others. The truly humble person will try to see how the sinful deeds done by others were committed because the person was unenlightened or misled, concluding that if the person had the same benefits and helps that he had, they would not have committed any such evil, but rather, would have done much good.

Saint Paul said of himself, "I am the chief of all sinners." This is how we should all view ourselves. But this rule is to be used with caution: do not say it to others, but keep it to yourself. Why? Because the reasons you have for feeling this way (the knowledge of your sins) is not known to others the way it is known to you, and it may make them doubt the praise you give to God for all he has done for you. If you keep these thoughts to yourself, you will be much more able to give God praise and thanks publicly.[21]

---

21. Richard J. Foster & James Bryan Smith, ed., *Devotional Classics: Selected Readings for Individuals and Groups* (New York, New York, HarperOne, 2005), p. 247.

111

Bible Wisdom: Jeremiah on Preparing for the Mission

FROM JEREMIAH 1:9–12

Then the LORD reached out his hand and touched my mouth and said to me, "I have put my words in your mouth. See, today I appoint you over nations and kingdoms to uproot and tear down, to destroy and overthrow, to build and to plant."

The word of the LORD came to me: "What do you see, Jeremiah?"

"I see the branch of an almond tree," I replied.

The LORD said to me, "You have seen correctly, for I am watching to see that my word is fulfilled."

112

The Power of Communion

For whenever you eat this bread and drink this cup,
you proclaim the Lord's death until he comes.

1 CORINTHIANS 11:26

You may call it Communion, the Lord's Supper, or the Eucharist. Your traditions indicate a specific way to receive this sacrament. Others may adapt different methods to accommodate the needs of their church community. But the fact remains that receiving the elements of bread and wine is a special moment between the Creator and those He has created. Receiving Christ into your life is nourishing and real. It is a recognition of what Christ did for us on the cross and a celebration of what He did for us when He rose from the grave. As we enter into this holy moment, we receive that which sustains us. Recognizing our dependence on Him creates a bond that is eternal. It's not just a ritual. It's a physical and spiritual interaction with God. It's a communal act that we enter into as a family. It's powerful when we join together as His people to receive His blessings. Come and open yourself up to God as He offers us food for the day. Has Communion become routine in your life? When is the last time you remembered the source of life?

113

The Power of Silence

He says, "Be still, and know that I am God; I will be exalted among the nations, I will be exalted in the earth."
PSALM 46:10

Silence is one of the hardest things you will ever try to achieve. We are so connected by a variety of devices. There's Wi-Fi at the coffee shop, at the library, and even in cars. Our smart phones and watches can do amazing things. We shop online and correspond via e-mail and text. We are addicted to staying connected. All these things make it even more difficult to find times of silence. To break away from checking our messages or watching videos is harder than it seems. But it is a quieting of the mind that can bring so much clarity. Once the electronic withdrawal has abated, you may be astounded at what fills your mind. You may experience long-forgotten memories, creative ideas, pain, or songs of praise. Trust God to fill your mind with the things that He needs you to release to Him. The good, the bad, and the ugly. These are the moments that can alter how you see the world and interact with those around you.

This is the nitty-gritty of getting real and surrendering it all to God. And you may never get there if you are too preoccupied with checking your messages. Trust me. Do the hard work of getting quiet before God. Are you willing to "go there?" It's worth it.

114

The Power of Fasting

"So that it will not be obvious to others that you are fasting,
but only to your Father, who is unseen; and your Father,
who sees what is done in secret, will reward you."
MATTHEW 6:18

What is fasting? For some folks, it seems like a crazy idea they only read about in the Bible. But fasting is yet another amazing tool that God has given us to know Him better.

Eating food, a daily activity that sustains life, does not seem like something that you should give up. And most of the time, eating a meal is very enjoyable. So if God created us to receive our daily nutrients through food, why would He want us to fast? It doesn't seem to make much sense. But for anyone who has entered into a time of prayer and fasting, you know that a fast is far more than just skipping a few meals. It is an intentional time of total reliance upon God, recognizing that He is the sustainer of life. As we replace food with prayer, our focus turns from ourselves to our Creator. Instead of self-reliance, we hand over control to God. And exercising the self-discipline to overcome hunger forces us to focus on our dependence on Him. And in that still, quiet moment, we enter into the presence of the Spirit. With distractions pushed aside, we can better hear from Him as He speaks to our lives. Devotional times become more vibrant as our prayers become so real.

Have you had this type of experience? Have you embraced this ancient practice of humbling yourself before the Lord?

115
The Power of Baptism

And the water symbolizes baptism that now saves you also—not the removal of dirt from the body but the pledge of a clear conscience toward God. It saves you by the resurrection of Jesus Christ.

1 PETER 3:21

Did you know that a lot people died fighting over baptism in sixteenth-century Germany? The Munster Rebellion raged during a time of unrest and economic struggles in the region. Proponents on both sides were passionate enough to die for their beliefs. The argument over who to baptize, when to baptize, and the methods of baptism was absorbed into a heated battle over government structure and distribution of wealth. Politics and power grabs turned a sacred act into a chaotic struggle. So let's learn from this little bit of church history and just stay focused on the spiritual beauty of baptism. Let's step away from the arguments of how and when and dwell on the gift of the sacrament. Baptism is a physical act that ushers in a spiritual reality. It is an act that represents our alliance with Christ. It is a recognition that He has forgiven our sins and we are dedicated to Him through the salvation that He offers.

We see in the Gospel of Mark that Jesus' ministry began only after He was baptized. A dove descended upon Him from heaven as God declared Jesus to be His Son, with whom He was pleased. Begin your ministry today. If you have never been baptized, follow His example and surrender to Him. If you have been baptized, step out in the assurance that you are His. In what ways can you remember your baptism today? What does it mean to be publically connected to God?

116

Eyewitness Encounter: "And the Holy Spirit Fell"

"But the Advocate, the Holy Spirit, whom the Father will send in my name, will teach you all things and will remind you of everything I have said to you."

JOHN 14:26

I'll never forget my first Christian concert. I was fourteen years old and staying in Florida with some family members for the summer. And since I wasn't old enough to drive, I had to go everywhere they went. I didn't know much about the Christian music scene. But I found myself at a Phil Driscoll concert. I wasn't looking forward to two hours of some guy playing the trumpet. But it turned out to be fantastic. I found myself totally enthralled by the music. At one point, I felt a strong wave of emotion as one of the songs came to its climax. I felt the Lord press upon my heart, and tears began to roll down my face. I looked around and noticed that others were also affected by the moment. The Holy Spirit filled the room and the music continued. We went well past the expected end of the concert as the full room praised God. It was a night that will forever be etched into my memory. I've had other moments where I felt the Spirit move, but nothing like that hot, humid night in Florida.

Christianity isn't always full of emotional highs. As a matter of fact, there are a lot of struggles and challenges. But there is no mistake when God moves and fills my heart with peace. I look forward to a day when I can praise Him without ceasing.

—**Melissa, Mom**

117

Spiritual Nudge: Brother Lawrence on Being Familiar with God

My heart, O God, is steadfast; I will sing and make music with all my soul. Awake, harp and lyre! I will awaken the dawn. I will praise you, LORD, among the nations; I will sing of you among the peoples.

PSALM 108:1–3

But when we are faithful in keeping ourselves in his holy presence, keeping him always before us, this not only prevents our offending him or doing something displeasing in his sight (at least willfully), but it also brings to us a holy freedom and if I may say so, a familiarity with God wherein we may ask and receive the graces we are so desperately in need of.

In short, by often repeating these acts they become habitual, and the presence of God becomes something that comes naturally to us. Give God thanks with me for his goodness toward me, which I can never sufficiently admire, and for the many favors he has done for so miserable a sinner as I am.[22]

---

22. Brother Lawrence, *The Practice of the Presence of God,* Translated by John J. Delaney (New York, New York, Doubleday, 1977).

118

Bible Wisdom: The Author of Hebrews on Faith

FROM HEBREWS 11:1–6

Now faith is confidence in what we hope for and assurance about what we do not see. This is what the ancients were commended for.

By faith we understand that the universe was formed at God's command, so that what is seen was not made out of what was visible.

By faith Abel brought God a better offering than Cain did. By faith he was commended as righteous, when God spoke well of his offerings. And by faith Abel still speaks, even though he is dead.

By faith Enoch was taken from this life, so that he did not experience death: "He could not be found, because God had taken him away." For before he was taken, he was commended as one who pleased God. And without faith it is impossible to please God, because anyone who comes to him must believe that he exists and that he rewards those who earnestly seek him.

119

My Prayer of Faith: Our Petitions to God

*"Therefore I tell you, whatever you ask for in prayer,
believe that you have received it, and it will be yours."*

MARK 11:24

These types of prayers are personal and intimate; they are the private conversations between ourselves and God. A prayer of faith can be expressed in a variety of ways: our specific requests, our many petitions, and our countless hopes and desires that we ask the Lord to bless and fulfill. . .if, of course, it is His will to do so.

The word *petition* means to ask for something. When our prayers are in line with God's will, we can be confident that He will hear and answer them. The Book of James tells us that a prayer of faith can heal the sick (5:15). Yet, as we make our appeals to God, we must (1) pray in faith, and (2) be prepared to wait.

God has promised to speak to our hearts, so we can expect Him to, and He will answer our specific prayers in line with His Word. However, the catalyst to receiving an answer from the Lord is our *faith*. (Take a moment to flip through the New Testament and count the number of times Jesus says to someone, "According to your faith.") When Jesus went to His hometown of Nazareth, scriptures say that He "did not do many miracles there because of their lack of faith" (Matthew 13:58).

Along with faith, we must be patient, because it can take time for God to speak. By causing us to wait, He prepares us for His answer, which we may have missed had He spoken immediately. And, likewise, we must be prepared to listen.

My Prayer of Faith:

_____

_____

120

My Prayers: "Lord, Hear These Words That Stem from My Faith in You. . ."

*Now faith is the assurance of things hoped for,
the conviction of things not seen.*
HEBREWS 11:1 ESV

My Petitions for My Family:

_____

_____

_____

My Petitions for My Friends:

_____

_____

_____

My Petitions for My Church:

_____

_____

_____

My Petitions for My Workplace:

_____

_____

_____

_____

PART FIVE

A Window into Their World

121

The World of a Child

*When Jesus saw this, he was indignant. He said to them,
"Let the little children come to me, and do not hinder them,
for the kingdom of God belongs to such as these."*
MARK 10:14

So many events fade out of our memories as the years go by. Our view of the world shifts from vivid scenes to shades of gray. The pictures in our mind dissolve into snapshots and short sound bites. And the world we once knew fades away. At times we only remember what we want. Other times we remember the things we wish we could forget. But the Lord calls us to remember what it is like to see the world with wonder and excitement. A world where we are protected, loved, and live free of worry and stress.

We didn't have to earn our way when we were younger. And work was just a chore or math problem. Our focus was our parents and siblings and classmates. There were no politics or power plays, just family and friends with all of their joys and frustrations. And some days ended with a big bowl of ice cream. As adults, we are pulled in so many directions at once that we lose our focus on our Father and forget the family of believers we have been born into. We need to stop and remember how much Jesus wants to take us in His arms, bless us, and give us His kingdom. He wants us to live with the hope of a child. When is the last time you spent time remembering your heavenly Father with childlike hope?

122

Get Down on the Floor

*Teach them to your children, talking about them when you
sit at home and when you walk along the road,
when you lie down and when you get up.*
DEUTERONOMY 11:19

We run, run, and run some more. We are so busy making life happen,
we often miss out on sharing ourselves with those we love. Life gets
quicker and quicker, and we seem to have so little time to spare in our
overscheduled days. The words of Deuteronomy instruct us to teach our
children all the things of God. They need to know that He is good, that
He loves us, and that He is mighty to save. So when do we accomplish
this during our busy days? We need to take a time-out. Sometimes, this
might mean you will have to get down on the floor and play. You could
hang out on the couch and play video games. Or you could go outside
and shoot some hoops. The goal is to connect with your family in their
own world. And other times, it can be fun to bring them into your world
as you go to work, the gym, or to see a movie. Just try to have some
spontaneous family fun that isn't on your to-do list and doesn't require
multitasking.

This formula for connecting with your family also works with
friends, neighbors, and coworkers. When you find you have time for the
important things (spending time with God, with your family, with others
in need) then your life will be complete—all the rest is just icing on the
cake.

123

Be a Loving Authority Figure

They disciplined us for a little while as they thought best; but God disciplines us for our good, in order that we may share in his holiness.
HEBREWS 12:10

Have you ever noticed how people change when they get behind the wheel of a car? Even the nicest people yell at other drivers, become judgmental, impatient, and short-tempered. Some others become timid and afraid, not willing to go onto highways and main roads where the speed limits are higher. Why? It has something to do with our perception of power. When we get in a car, we have a lethal weapon in our hands and the freedom to drive recklessly, if we choose. You can tell a lot about a person by the way they drive. It's a small insight into their perceptions of power and personal responsibility.

The same is true when people suddenly find themselves in a position of authority. With the freedom to build companies, organizations, churches and families the way they want, people can become self-centered and controlling. Instead, we should all desire to build loving and nurturing atmospheres with room and opportunity for everyone to grow. So how do you drive? Do you have the humility it takes to be a loving authority figure?

124

Don't Forget Why You Are There

*How beautiful on the mountains are the feet of those who bring good
news, who proclaim peace, who bring good tidings, who proclaim
salvation, who say to Zion, "Your God reigns!"*

ISAIAH 52:7

I feel like I'm being tugged and pulled in so many different directions.
I am the keeper of the kids' schedules, I help with homework, I take the
car in for oil changes, I have a job, I take night classes, I occasionally
enjoy a night out with my husband, and I also volunteer at church.
Sometimes I feel like too many people depend on me. I hardly get a
chance to stop and think about why I do some of the things I do. If I
stopped being all things to all people, I would have a huge mess to clean
up, right? I must admit that sometimes I serve others out of obligation.
I show up because it's what I have always done. But lately I have found
great comfort in remembering why I dedicate a portion of my time to
volunteering. God reigns, and I am on His team. He loves every person
out there, and He has chosen me to help spread His blessings. Knowing
that I play a significant role in His mission motivates me to serve. Have
you forgotten why you serve? Have you thanked Him today for bringing
you into His mission?

125

Eyewitness Encounter: "I Learned More from My Class Than They Did from Me"

Each of you should use whatever gift you have received to serve others, as faithful stewards of God's grace in its various forms.

1 PETER 4:10

I've grown up in the church. I am very comfortable teaching a class of adults or children. I've worked in the nursery. I have coordinated the lights for musicals, cleaned the gym, chaperoned youth trips, and done almost every other job in the church. So when my Sunday school teacher asked me to be the substitute teacher one week, I gladly accepted. She provided me the scripture reference and the topic of discussion and told me to just go for it. The topic was Communion. I prepared my lesson and was ready for class. It went well and everyone seemed engaged. But during the discussion portion of the class, some folks began to ask some really hard questions. I navigated it well, and everyone seemed to be reflective and open. But inside, I was second-guessing myself. Who was I to teach a Sunday school class? What if my responses were incorrect? Later, I connected those in the class with questions to another leader who had devoted a lot of time to our topic of discussion. I also passed their questions on to the regular teacher, and she was able to continue the discussion for several weeks.

Even though I was a little insecure about my abilities, I was able to get help from many others for those adults around the table. It took teamwork and humility, but in the end, God was glorified and we all grew closer to Him. I know I was the teacher that day, but I sure did learn a lot from my classmates.

—**Louis, Volunteer**

126

Spiritual Nudge: Hannah Whitall Smith on Entire Control

"This is the covenant I will establish with the people of Israel after that time, declares the LORD. I will put my laws in their minds and write them on their hearts. I will be their God, and they will be my people. No longer will they teach their neighbor, or say to one another, 'Know the Lord,' because they will all know me, from the least of them to the greatest. For I will forgive their wickedness and will remember their sins no more."

HEBREWS 8:6–13

What you need to do, then, dear Christian, if you are in bondage in the matter of service, is to put your will over completely into the hands of your Lord, surrendering to Him the entire control of it. Say, "Yes, Lord, yes!" to everything, and trust Him so to work in you to will, as to bring your whole wishes and affections into conformity with His own sweet, and lovable, and most lovely will.

I have seen this done often in cases where it looked beforehand an utterly impossible thing. In one case, where a lady had been for years rebelling fearfully against a little act of service which she knew was right, but which she hated, I saw her, out of the depths of despair, and without any feeling whatever, give her will in that matter up into the hands of her Lord, and begin to say to Him, *"Thy will be done!"* And in one short hour that very thing began to look sweet and precious to her.[23]

---

23. Hannah Whitall Smith, *The Christian's Secret of a Happy Life* (New Kensington, Pennsylvania, Whitaker House, 1983).

127

Bible Wisdom: Christ on Loving One Another

From John 13:31–38

When he was gone, Jesus said, "Now the Son of Man is glorified and God is glorified in him. If God is glorified in him, God will glorify the Son in himself, and will glorify him at once.

"My children, I will be with you only a little longer. You will look for me, and just as I told the Jews, so I tell you now: Where I am going, you cannot come.

"A new command I give you: Love one another. As I have loved you, so you must love one another. By this everyone will know that you are my disciples, if you love one another."

Simon Peter asked him, "Lord, where are you going?"

Jesus replied, "Where I am going, you cannot follow now, but you will follow later."

Peter asked, "Lord, why can't I follow you now? I will lay down my life for you."

Then Jesus answered, "Will you really lay down your life for me? Very truly I tell you, before the rooster crows, you will disown me three times!"

128

The Tricky Teen Years

Flee the evil desires of youth and pursue righteousness, faith, love and peace, along with those who call on the Lord out of a pure heart.
2 TIMOTHY 2:22

One year they set up a huge obstacle course at church camp. We were all excited, or nervous, as we lined up across the lawn to try our prowess at maneuvering through the obstacles. We were given good direction before we began, but we seemed to forget it all once we were on the course. All we wanted to do was be the fastest and best. Without fail, it was a comical disaster. We got stuck at the ropes wall, stumbled through the tires on the ground, and spent most of our time and energy trying to get back up after falling down. But some people were so focused on beating this thing, they volunteered to go twice. And the second time through, most of them did much better, because they had learned some key tricks the first time around.

It's too bad we can't go back and relive our teen years. We would be able to better navigate our way through the fears, inadequacies, and missteps of youth. I bet we would all do so much better. Hindsight would make it so much easier to avoid bad decisions and selfish desires. We would spend more time on the things that matter.

We can't go back, but we can help those who are going through the process of young adulthood today. The teen years are tricky for every generation. Do you remember what it was like for you? Are you there for a teenager who is trying to find his or her place in the world?

129
Those Giggly Girls

A cheerful heart is good medicine,
but a crushed spirit dries up the bones.
PROVERBS 17:22

When I was a kid, almost everyone I knew had two paintings of Jesus. One was of Him knocking at the proverbial door. And the other depicted Him with children sitting at His feet as He spoke. The kids seemed so quiet and peaceful. But even as a child, I knew that this was not how kids acted. This image seemed like the wishful product of adults everywhere: children who would sit quietly and listen when spoken to.

The reality is that kids are full of energy and have very short attention spans. I think those kids who Jesus spoke with in the scriptures were probably regular kids who were giggling, running, playing, jumping around, and trying to whisper to each other. They may have even gotten into an argument over who won their game of tag. They were just kids.

I know it's important for kids to learn to be respectful during church, but we should not zap our kids' zest for life. Let the girls giggle. Let the boys run. Let's let our kids enjoy being with their church family. The Lord fills us with unspeakable joy, and He has created us with the capacity to share that joy with those around us. So find joy in the giggly girl. She is just expressing the life God has given her. When's the last time you stopped and shared in her exuberance?

130

Children Need Men and Women Leaders

So the next generation would know them, even the children
yet to be born, and they in turn would tell their children.
PSALM 78:6

The Israelites were divided up into clans—family lines that lived, moved, ate, and worshiped together. They owned property together and took care of each other on a daily basis, especially if there was a tragedy or death. Orphaned children were absorbed into their extended family so that everyone was protected and safe.

Today the cultural trend is to take care of our family only when it is convenient, and as a result, many are orphaned and neglected in times of need. Our tendency is to believe that as long as children are fed, clothed, and sheltered, their basic needs have been met. But in the absence of adequate parental guidance, boys and girls need other strong men and women in their lives to lead them. Being fed is not the same as being led. . .or loved. . .or nurtured. Can we, as a church, fill the gap for young people in need? Are you being called to be the trustworthy, nurturing surrogate of a lonely child's heart and soul?

131

Partner with the Parents

"At that time," declares the LORD, "I will be the God
of all the families of Israel, and they will be my people."
JEREMIAH 31:1

Parents can't always do it alone. It's tough to raise a child, even in the healthiest of families that love and support one another. It can be difficult to instill love, knowledge, and compassion into a young new life. But our Creator knows this and has given us our church family. He is our ultimate partner in parenthood as He brings us together in diverse local communities of faith. We don't have all the answers on our own, and we can't peek into the future. But God knows and loves each one of us. So whether we are adults, infants, or somewhere in between, we have His promise that He will always be there for us. Do the families in your congregation share life together? Do other adults share in the responsibility of teaching the children? Are you a part of this process?

Eyewitness Encounter: "I Almost Missed Out"

Thanks be to God for His indescribable gift!
2 CORINTHIANS 9:15

I used to play in a classic rock 'n' roll band. I enjoyed the arduous task of putting together a set list and practicing with my bandmates. Playing music was a labor of love, and every show was a rush of adrenaline. But then something happened. I met Christ. The woman I was dating was a believer, and she invited me to church. I liked her and I was curious about church, so I attended. I did not expect the Spirit of God to grab me about two weeks later during worship. I surrendered my life to Him. I saw and felt things I hadn't before. I was a grown man experiencing a life that I didn't even know existed just a few weeks prior. As time passed, the secular band I was part of now felt shallow and empty. Soon, I was asked to audition for a worship team at church. I distinctly remember the Lord telling me, "You can't have both. Choose." So I chose worship.

My heart longed to go deeper, and I eventually left my rock band altogether. I dove into worship. Little did I know that my small act of obedience would bestow God's anointing on my life. Even now, twenty years later, I am honored to be able to lead people into the presence of God. I am thankful for the gift He has given me.

—**Walter, Worship Leader**

Spiritual Nudge:
Dietrich Bonhoeffer on Community

By setting aside in his flesh the law with its commands and
regulations. His purpose was to create in himself one new humanity
out of the two, thus making peace, and in one body to reconcile both of
them to God through the cross, by which he put to death their hostility.
EPHESIANS 2:15–16

The fact that we are brethren only through Jesus Christ is of immeasurable significance. Not only the other person who is earnest and devout, who come to me seeking brotherhood, must I deal with in fellowship. My brother is rather that other person who has been redeemed by Christ, delivered from sin, and called to faith and eternal life.

Not what a man is in himself as a Christian, his spirituality and piety, constitutes the basis of our community. What determines our brotherhood is what that man is by reason of Christ. Our community with one another consists soley in what Christ has done to both of us. This is true not merely at the beginning, and though in the course of time something else were to be added to our community; it remains so for all the future and to all eternity.

I have community with others and I shall continue to have it only through Jesus Christ. The more genuine and the deeper our community becomes, the more will everything else between us recede, the more clearly and purely will Jesus Christ and his work become the one and only thing that is vital between us. We have one another only through Christ, but through Christ we do have one another, wholly, and for all eternity.[24]

---

24. Dietrich Bonhoeffer, *Life Together* (New York, New York, HarperOne, 1954), pp. 25-26.

134

Bible Wisdom: David on the Rock for All Generations

FROM PSALM 144:1–10

Praise be to the LORD my Rock,
who trains my hands for war,
my fingers for battle.
He is my loving God and my fortress,
my stronghold and my deliverer,
my shield, in whom I take refuge,
who subdues peoples under me.

LORD, what are human beings that you care for them,
mere mortals that you think of them?
They are like a breath; their days are like a fleeting shadow.

Part your heavens, LORD, and come down;
touch the mountains, so that they smoke.
Send forth lightning and scatter the enemy;
shoot your arrows and rout them.
Reach down your hand from on high;
deliver me and rescue me
from the mighty waters,
from the hands of foreigners
whose mouths are full of lies,
whose right hands are deceitful.

I will sing a new song to you, my God;
one the ten-stringed lyre I will make music to you,
to the One who gives victory to kings,
who delivers his servant David.

135

Why Small Group Ministry Is So Important

If either of them falls down, one can help the other up. But pity
anyone who falls and has no one to help them up.
ECCLESIASTES 4:10

We were created to live in community with one another. The Word of God gives us many examples of how we are all a part of one body. We are members of the kingdom that He created, designed, and continues to build over time. There are no Lone Rangers in the Spirit, although sometimes it feels that way. When we don't intentionally engage with those Christ has placed in our lives, we can't benefit from the gifts they have to offer. If others have hurt us, we can find ourselves in a lonely and discouraging place. It's easy to fall through the cracks.

If you look around your church on any given Sunday, you will find yourself surrounded by people who are seeking to connect with God and with others. It may not appear that way, but it's true. Sometimes, those who are volunteering as greeters, teachers, and ushers are the only people who interact with individuals attending services. This is why small group connections are so important. We are encouraged, even commanded, by the Lord to gather together and encourage one another, pray for each other, confess our sins, accept healing, and share the talents the Lord has given to each of us. Extend your service to others through small groups and make some God-inspired connections.

136

It's Okay to Have Fun

A person can do nothing better than to eat and drink and find satisfaction in their own toil. This too, I see, is from the hand of God.
ECCLESIASTES 2:24

Do you realize how much God wants us to be happy? Why do you think He hates sin so much? It's because sin steals our joy and brings misery, distress, and death. God doesn't want us to suffer. He knows that we live in a broken world and that life can be hard, but it is never His desire for us to hurt. The Lord created this world—and us. And it was perfect before we turned our backs on Him to try and go our own way.

Before sin entered into our reality, there weren't broken relationships and strife. But sin happened, and now we must place our hope in Him, because He is the one who wants to bring us back into harmony with Himself and the rest of creation. Our work for Him was supposed to be enjoyable. Serving others was supposed to come naturally and be mutually beneficial. Our labor was supposed to be followed by a day of rest and reflection. We were never supposed to be separated from God, and He is constantly reaching out and offering us redemption so we can reconnect with Him and all He has to offer. His joy is for today as much as it is for our future. So have some fun the next time you volunteer—it's okay. Try to think of your life's work as a celebration of the talents He has given you.

137

Be Available

Greater love has no one than this:
to lay down one's life for one's friends.
JOHN 15:13

We are called to lay down our lives. This is hard to do. Yet Jesus told us that we should take His yoke upon us because His yoke is easy and His burden is light. How can both be right? Can this paradox be resolved this side of heaven?

There is a key to this verse that is often missed. We frequently feel like we are letting God down if we are not always available to others. But this can lead to exhaustion and burnout because we misunderstand what it means to *be available*. It doesn't mean that we must say yes every time someone asks us to do something. It means that we are supposed to be available to God when He calls us to action. If we open up to Him, He will interact with us throughout the day. His voice and touch will guide us as we learn to follow his lead.

Sometimes we will hear a gentle voice, and other times it will be urgent. But if we tune our ears to pick up on God's signals, no matter how quietly and softly they come to us, we are laying down our lives daily for Him. And this is the daily sacrifice that is needed for the Holy Spirit to reach the lost and fallen world around us. Are you available to Him?

138

Ministering with Your Church Family

"In the same way, let your light shine before others, that they may see your good deeds and glorify your Father in heaven."
MATTHEW 5:16

Do you remember a childhood story about a prince and princess that didn't know they were royalty? They always knew in their hearts that they were meant for more and lived with this nagging feeling that they were displaced somehow. For some dramatic reason, they were safely tucked away to keep their identities hidden from the bad guys. So they worked hard and hoped for a brighter future. But they had no idea that their rightful place was to lead their country. The story gets even better when they discover their true identities and reclaim their birthright.

Believe it or not, this story is pretty similar to our own lives. As a child of the Living God, do you know what your birthright is? Did you know that you are qualified to share in the inheritance of the saints because you are His child? He has made us, His Church, a royal priesthood. We are the children of the Most High, who has given us everything. As we minister together and fulfill the work He has given us here on earth, remember that we are a part of an eternal kingdom. Do you know your worth? Have you accepted your place in His royal court?

139

Eyewitness Encounter: "Training the Trainer"

So Christ himself gave the apostles, the prophets, the evangelists,
the pastors and the teachers, to equip his people for the works
of service, so that the body of Christ may be built up.
EPHESIANS 4:11–12

I have been in the classroom for many years as both a student and a teacher. But one of my favorite things is to train the trainers. It is a special task to help others who share a desire to be trainers. It's exciting to foster the love of teaching in others. But just like any classroom, some students are just difficult. People are wired so differently that simple communication can sometimes be next to impossible. Sure, it's easy to be with those who are just like me. I love it when folks get my stories, cultural references, and jokes, and it can be exhausting to be with those who look at me like I'm crazy. But it is so important to remember that we are all a part of God's plan. All the different personalities and temperaments fit into the larger picture, and we all have value in God's eyes. I have learned to accept the challenge of helping those unlike myself to find the voice that God has given them. Covering each session in prayer and gathering up as much patience as I can is a winning combination to connect with those who are nothing like me.

—Vanessa, Sunday School Coordinator

140

Spiritual Nudge: Isaac Penington on a Tender Hand

"My command is this:
Love each other as I have loved you."
JOHN 15:12

Oh! Wait to feel this spirit. Wait to be guided and to walk in this spirit that you may enjoy the Lord in sweetness and walk meekly, tenderly, peaceably, and lovingly with one another. Then you will be able to praise the Lord, and anything that has hindered you, you will be able to overcome in the Lamb's dominion. That which is contrary shall be trampled upon as his life rises and begins to rule in you.

So, watch your hearts and ways. Watch over one another in gentleness and tenderness. Know that we cannot help one another out of a snare of our own strength, for only the Lord, who must be waited upon, can do this in all and for all. So, attend to the Truth, to the service and enjoyment and possession of it in your hearts. Walk in such a way that you do not bring disgrace upon it, but instead, let the Truth be a good savor to others in the places where you live. May the meek, innocent, tender, righteous life that reigns within you and governs you, shine through you into the eyes of all when you speak.[25]

25. Isaac Penington, *The Works of Isaac Penington* (Philadelphia, Pennsylvania, Friends Book Store, 1863).

141

Bible Wisdom:
The Author of Hebrews on Meeting Together

FROM HEBREWS 10:19–25

Therefore, brothers and sisters, since we have confidence to enter the Most Holy Place by the blood of Jesus, by a new and living way opened for us through the curtain, that is, his body, and since we have a great priest over the house of God, let us draw near to God with a sincere heart and with the full assurance that faith brings, having our hearts sprinkled to cleanse us from a guilty conscience and having our bodies washed with pure water. Let us hold unswervingly to the hope we profess, for he who promised is faithful. And let us consider how we may spur one another on toward love and good deeds, not giving up meeting together, as some are in the habit of doing, but encouraging one another—and all the more as you see the Day approaching.

142

Multigenerational Ministry

*"And through your offspring all nations on earth
will be blessed, because you have obeyed me."*
GENESIS 22:18

Some things are just in your genes. You can't change them. There are wonderful talents like writing, musical gifts, athletic ability, intelligence, wisdom, beauty, and kindness. Some other traits aren't so wonderful and become obstacles that we have to navigate throughout our life. Generation after generation, we either build or lose those qualities that have been given to us. We learn from one another as we live and serve together. Different generations learning and volunteering side by side brings wholeness to our lives. And it is the best way to pass on the talents we have been given.

Long before our society was accustomed to age-based learning, individuals of all ages lived, worked, served, and worshiped together. Talents and blessings were shared. And people of all ages learned from one another. When is the last time you served alongside someone from a different age group? Have you encouraged the young people in your life to volunteer?

143

Seeing the World through the Eyes of a Widow

Rejoice with those who rejoice; mourn with those who mourn.
ROMANS 12:15

Susan stood in the middle of the car lot gazing over rows of new vehicles in every color and size. The thought of buying a new car was overwhelming. But as the salesman approached, she knew she had to seem nonchalant and only half-interested. This was the first time in over forty years that she had shopped for a car all by herself. Her husband had passed away three years ago, and she was in desperate need of a new car. So there she stood, playing it cool, while she secretly shook inside. The entire process reminded her that she was all alone. She had no one physically in her life to share decisions with. But she had God. She had relearned how to rely on Him and His comfort. She rediscovered the power of prayer as she sought to make the big decisions on her own. And she had allowed those in her faith community into her life. That is why God has called us to care for the widows. It's our job to let them know that they are not alone. Have you intentionally reached out to a widow or widower lately?

144

Young Adults: Caught in the Middle

But the LORD said to me, "Do not say, 'I am too young.' You must go to everyone I send you to and say whatever I command you. Do not be afraid of them, for I am with you and will rescue you," declares the LORD.
JEREMIAH 1:7–8

Our identity is everything to us. It affects everything we think, do, and say. Every single decision we make comes from who we believe ourselves to be or who we believe we are not. As young adults we are caught in the middle of some of our most significant life changes. We are shedding the world as we know it, leaving the safety of childhood, and venturing out on our own. We no longer have our food, shelter, school, and entertainment provided for us by the adults in our lives. We take on the responsibilities of earning a paycheck and paying the bills. We must figure out taxes, contracts, and politics on our own. This significant change does not come easily or quickly. Do we shy away in fear. . .or do we go after it, guns blazing?

Like never before, it's important to know that the Lord loves us and has prepared a way for us at this precarious stage of life. He wants to walk with us as we find our place within our faith community and discover ways to share our talents with others. It becomes up to us to serve Him without being told to do so. It's a wonderful time of exploration and discovery. So be brave as you seek your place in His kingdom.

145
Act Like a Kid

"Whoever welcomes one of these little children in my name welcomes me; and whoever welcomes me does not welcome me but the one who sent me."

MARK 9:37

I grew up in the church. I was one of those kids that ran around the church building like it was my own house. We spent hours playing hide-and-seek, tag, and scouting in and around the building. We knew all of the best hiding places and secret passages. I can even remember climbing on the scaffolding when we were building a new sanctuary. The church was a safe and fun place where we learned about God and shared our lives with each other. We knew that we were welcomed there. We knew that the teachers, coaches, and preachers were devoted to helping us know God.

But sometimes I lose some of these feelings for the church. After dealing with disappointments and difficult people, it can be hard to appreciate the joy of the children who now run through the church halls laughing and playing. I am part of a loving and committed community of believers. And only when I intentionally set aside the stresses of adulthood can I jump in and enjoy my time at church. Just like the kids running and playing, I can rekindle the joy of being with others who bask in God's freedom by letting go of all the trivial things holding me back.

146

Eyewitness Encounter: "God Made Us a Family for a Reason"

"The King will reply, 'Truly I tell you, whatever you did for one of the least of these brothers and sisters of mine, you did for me.'"
MATTHEW 25:40

I'm a single mom. And I can tell you firsthand how important my church family is to me and my son. I've heard a lot of sermons on how we are to reach the "least of these" on the outskirts of our faith communities. We are to serve those who are naked, lonely, and hungry. Jesus instructed us to care for the widows and orphans. We need to connect with those who are immobile and unable to come to church on their own. I totally agree with this mission. But I am also very aware of the need for internal ministry. There are so many different kinds of "prisons" that have entrapped people. Addictions and loneliness are all around us.

As the members of Christ's Body, we are to care first for our fellow members. While that single mom and her children are clothed and fed, they may still be struggling on the inside. It's hard to sit in a pew by yourself week after week, year after year. Service to the body isn't hard—it's about making yourself a friend to the friendless, gently anticipating needs, and listening. From one of the "least of these," I can tell you, it's why God made us a family.

—**Melba, Single Mom**

147

Spiritual Nudge: Holly Catterton Allen and Christine Lawton Ross on Intergenerational Christian Formation

Therefore let us move beyond the elementary teachings about Christ and be taken forward to maturity, not laying again the foundation of repentance from acts that lead to death, and of faith in God.

HEBREWS 6:1

Throughout Scripture God tells his people to remember his mighty acts and to tell the next generations of his power and the wonders he has done (Psalm 78:4). Several times in scripture, specific illustrations of how to do this are laid out. For example, when the Israelites crossed the Jordan into the Promised Land, Joshua instructed that a stone altar be built with twelve stones, representing the twelve tribes. Then Joshua said, "When your children ask their fathers in times to come, 'What do these stones mean?' then you shall let your children know, 'Israel passed over this Jordan on dry ground.' For the LORD your God dried up the waters of the Jordan for you until you passed over…so that all the peoples of the earth may know that the hand of the LORD is mighty, that you may fear the LORD your God forever" (Joshua 4:21–24 ESV).

The way that the Israelites were to tell the next generations about God was to describe for them what God had done in their lives. Those stories were written down—they are the Bible stories we tell today—and as Sandage, Aubrey and Ohland say, "As essential purpose of the church is to be a community of memory that tells and retells God's larger transcending story." However, we are not only to be telling the stories of how God worked in the past; we are also to tell our children and the next generations about God's ongoing work in the world today. One of the best ways to do this is to tell about God's mighty acts in our own lives: "The Christian community. . .embedding one's personal story in a larger story is [an important]…dimension of community."[26]

148

Bible Wisdom:
The Author of Acts on Saul's Conversion

FROM ACTS 9:26–31

When he came to Jerusalem, he tried to join the disciples, but they were all afraid of him, not believing that he really was a disciple. But Barnabas took him and brought him to the apostles. He told them how Saul on his journey had seen the Lord and that the Lord had spoken to him, and how in Damascus he had preached fearlessly in the name of Jesus. So Saul stayed with them and moved about freely in Jerusalem, speaking boldly in the name of the Lord. He talked and debated with the Hellenistic Jews, but they tried to kill him. When the believers learned of this, they took him down to Caesarea and sent him off to Tarsus.

Then the church throughout Judea, Galilee and Samaria enjoyed a time of peace and was strengthened. Living in fear of the Lord and encouraged by the Holy Spirit, it increased in numbers.

---

26. Holly Catterton Allen & Christine Lawton Ross, *Intergenerational Christian Formation: Bringing the Whole Church Together in Ministry, Community and Worship* (Downers Grove, Illinois, IVP Academic, 2012) pp. 219-220.

149

My Prayer of Agreement: United in Cause

"Again, truly I tell you that if two of you on earth agree about anything you ask for, it will be done for them by my Father in heaven. For where two or three gather in my name, there am I with them."
MATTHEW 18:19–20

When Jesus introduced this type of prayer, He made it clear that in order for it to be effective, those praying must be in agreement.

So if two people are in perfect harmony with one another on a specific prayer request—essentially praying for the exact same thing—there is extreme power in their unity, and the faith, compassion, and commitment of these Christ-followers can move the hand of God.

While the Lord wants our daily one-on-one time with Him to be a priority, there are definite moments when united group prayer should be our focus. For example, when my mother was involved in a head-on collision while driving on a windy mountain road, my family and friends quickly joined each other in prayer. We were most definitely in agreement, interceding for my mom's health, safety, and well-being.

I've learned firsthand that powerful, focused prayers of agreement can result in miracles.

My Prayer of Agreement

_____

_____

_____

_____

150

My Prayers: "Lord, Hear These Prayers That We Share. . ."

But the wisdom that comes from heaven is first of all pure; then peace-loving, considerate, submissive, full of mercy and good fruit, impartial and sincere. Peacemakers who sow in peace raise a harvest of righteousness.
JAMES 3:17–18

My Prayer of Agreement for My Family:
_____
_____
_____

My Prayer of Agreement for My Friends:
_____
_____
_____

My Prayer of Agreement for My Church:
_____
_____
_____

My Prayer of Agreement for My Workplace:
_____
_____
_____

PART SIX

Rx for Weary Workers

151

I'm Burned Out?

"Take my yoke upon you and learn from me, for I am gentle and humble in heart, and you will find rest for your souls."
MATTHEW 11:29

Do you ever get to the point that you feel you're losing your mind? Like those times that you can't remember what day it is? Or when you walk in a room and you can't remember why? I recently heard a graduate student describe how it felt to read some of her work from when she first began her studies. She said it had depth and was full of creativity. But when she compared it to her most recent work, she was disappointed in herself. Her final papers were routine and repetitive. She had always expected her studies would grow toward the end of her degree. But instead, they were less inspired.

This is a sign of burnout. It happens in ministry all the time. We sometimes choose to serve out of a personal sense of duty or because there is no one else to do the job. But overextending ourselves can zap our creativity. Inspiration fades in the throes of responsibility. There is a reason God gave us the Sabbath. We function at our best when we are well rested. It's how we are designed. So take a huge tip from our Creator and take a day off. It is the most responsible thing you can do sometimes.

152

Is It Okay to Take a Break?

"Six days you shall labor, but on the seventh day you shall rest;
even during the plowing season and harvest you must rest."
EXODUS 34:21

"You deserve a break today!" was a popular slogan in the 1980s. Sure, it was designed to sell candy bars, but it got the American public's attention. "Go, go, go," is the message we usually hear. It was kind of nice to hear that we deserve a break. It's certainly not a message we usually hear from our churches. Sermon after sermon urges us to reach our world through loving service. And that is a good call to action. There are hungry kids, lonely people, and lost souls. And God has chosen the Church as His method of reaching those folks. But you don't have to carry the burden of a lost world on your shoulders alone. It is a collective effort among all of His people. No one person is instructed to perform all tasks associated with reaching a hurting world. God designed us to be a part of a community. And in this community, there are many different people with many different talents who come together to worship the one true God. Our efforts in this broken world are supposed to be collective. So don't take a break from compassion, but feel free to step aside from time to time to allow someone else to head up the mission.

153

Finding Your Place

We have different gifts, according to the grace given to each of us.
If your gift is prophesying, then prophesy in accordance with your faith;
if it is serving, then serve; if it is teaching, then teach; if it is to encourage,
then give encouragement; if it is giving, then give generously; if it is
to lead, do it diligently; if it is to show mercy, do it cheerfully.
ROMANS 12:6–8

Take a moment to google the topic of "spiritual gifts test." You may be surprised to find the many different test questionnaires that have been created to help people discover their talents. Some of these tests are more extensive than others. But they have all been developed as tools to help the average person identify their talents. I recommend that you take one or two of these tests. You may be surprised by the results. Or they may reinforce what you already know about yourself. If you are standing back wondering how to help others, or which Sunday school class to teach, or if you should try out for the worship team at church, one of these assessments might help you out. With this self-knowledge you can then take the steps to try out some different areas of service. Volunteer here and there until you find the right fit. Most volunteer groups and pastors will appreciate your intentional search for the right fit. And when you find the place that excites you and sparks your creativity, then you can jump in with both feet. And the experience you have gained through the process will only help you better understand the bigger picture of your church or organization. So, what's your talent? Have you put it into action?

154
Dream Big

"And afterword, I will pour out my Spirit on all people.
Your sons and daughters will prophesy, your old men
will dream dreams, your young men will see visions."
JOEL 2:28

A few years back I attended a school reunion. It was great to see old friends and meet their families. We sat around and told stories about how crazy we were in school and all the stupid things we did. The organizers had requested that we all bring photos to the reunion. As we sat around a big table and took time to look at each other's photos, I noticed a big difference between some of the collections. Some people only brought photos from their school days. Others brought photos of their young adult years after school. And others brought photos of their current life. Soon, the conversation turned to our hopes and dreams. I noticed that there was a collation between people's dreams and their photo albums. Those who only brought photos from school only talked about how they wished they were still in school. Likewise the folks who only brought recent photos only spoke of what they wanted to do in the future. These varying perspectives said a lot about people's dreams. Some were caught in the past while others only focused on the future. So which is the better perspective? I believe it is a combination of both. Our past experiences shape who we are today. And our hope for the future is where we live out those dreams. So hold on to the past, but don't forget to dream big about all the new adventures you will have tomorrow.

155

Eyewitness Encounter: "I Ran Till My Legs Fell Off"

Not only so, but we also glory in our sufferings,
because we know that suffering produces perseverance;
perseverance, character; and character, hope.
ROMANS 5:3–4

I tried to think of something else. I looked to the horizon and leaned forward. I breathed in through my nose and out through my mouth. My lungs burned. My arms seemed to be on autopilot as they thrust back and forth. My legs felt like melting rubber. I knew I had to keep going. This was a test of endurance. I kept telling myself that it was all a mental game and I was not going to stop. Somehow, I was moving past the pain. I was operating on a whole new level. I was going to finish the race.

Sometimes, life feels like a marathon. I use the same tactics as a long-distance runner to keep moving from event to event. I can't stop. I must fight through the discomfort. But in life, my strength doesn't come from within. It comes from my Creator who is my sustainer. It's okay to run till my legs fall off, because I know that He will provide for my needs. And He cares for me enough to give me a day of rest every week. Thank You, God, for endurance and rest. You are so good to me!

—Jason, Avid Runner

156

Spiritual Nudge: George Fox on The Bright Morning Star

"Shout it aloud, do not hold back. Raise your voice like a trumpet. Declare to my people their rebellion and to the descendants of Jacob their sins."

ISAIAH 58:1

All dear Friends everywhere, who have no helper but the Lord, who is your strength and your life, let your cries and prayers be to him, who with his eternal power has kept your heads above all waves and storms. Let none go out of their habitations in the stormy time of the night, those whose habitation is the Lord, the Seed, Christ Jesus.

In this Seed you will see the bright and morning Star appear which will expel the night of darkness, by which morning Star you will come to the everlasting Day which was before night was. So, everyone feel this bright morning Star in your hearts, there to expel the darkness.[27]

157

Bible Wisdom: Job on Trusting God

FROM JOB 42:1–6

Then Job replied to the LORD:
    "I know that you can do all things;
        no purpose of yours can be thwarted.

---

27. Richard J. Foster & James Bryan Smith, ed., *Devotional Classics: Selected Readings for Individuals and Groups* (New York, New York, HarperOne, 2005). Page 189.

You asked, 'Who is this that obscures my plans without knowledge?'
    Surely I spoke of things I did not understand,
    things too wonderful for me to know.

"You said, 'Listen now, and I will speak;
    I will question you,
    and you shall answer me.'
My ears had heard of you
    but now my eyes have seen you.
Therefore I despise myself
    and repent in dust and ashes."

158

Reevaluating Your Ministry

*There is a time for everything, and a season
for every activity under the heavens.*
ECCLESIASTES 3:1

There is a time for everything. We have all heard the song and read the scripture about the different phases of life. It's good to remember this when we are having a hard time letting go of the good or bad things we have experienced in the past. Along the way, most of us have learned to reevaluate our lives and move forward. But it seems very hard to do this when it comes to ministry. We sometimes hold so tightly to what worked for us, or a family member, that we miss new opportunities that are right in front of us. Maybe VBS needs to be replaced with Sports Camp. Maybe we should have a mix of hymns and praise choruses in our worship. Maybe the pews need to be replaced with moveable chairs to increase flexibility for special events. Or maybe we should rotate volunteers monthly instead of quarterly. There are so many different ways to minister to people. We don't have to keep an existing structure just because it served us well in the past. Maybe it's time to step back and brainstorm new ways to reach others. What changes can you make to reach more people? What programs can you institute to take care of your volunteers?

159

The Right People at the Right Time

Have nothing to do with the fruitless deeds of darkness, but rather expose them.
EPHESIANS 5:11

I once heard a missionary tell a story about the scariest night of his life. He lived in a remote village in southern Africa with his wife. On a stormy night, two thieves broke into their home. As he resisted them, one of the thieves shot him in the stomach. They then took their valuables and fled into the storm. Because of the thunder, no one heard the shots. But he didn't want his wife to run for help because he feared the thieves might still be nearby. However, a local man had been out checking the fences around the village. He didn't usually go by the missionary's house, but the storm had washed out one of the roads and he had to go a different route. When the missionary and his wife saw his headlights, she ran to his vehicle in desperation. They were able to load the missionary in the back of the pickup and get him to a doctor. His life was saved, and the couple was able to stay in the country they had grown to love.

This is an extreme example of the right person being in the right place at the right time. Where is God leading you? Does it seem as crazy as going out into a dark stormy night to check a fence? God's ways are often mysterious. It's our job to just trust and obey. We are all a part of His bigger plan.

160

It's Okay to Push

*For I testify that they gave as much as they were able,
and even beyond their ability. Entirely on their own.*
2 CORINTHIANS 8:3

David was so excited to make the junior varsity basketball team. He had practiced all summer and lived with a basketball in his hands. He had pushed himself during tryouts, and it paid off. He was on the team. But once practice began, he noticed that he was in over his head. He knew how to play, but the physical strength and ability of the other players far exceeded his. He worked and worked but just couldn't perform. His coach kept calling him out and yelling for him to work harder. He made him do extra drills, run more laps, do more push-ups, and shoot more shots. David was exhausted and frustrated. He wanted to quit. But he didn't. As he stepped onto the court for the first game, he was nervous that so many people were getting ready to watch him fail. But the opposite happened. He ran, shot, rebounded, and played better than he had before. He was unstoppable. After the game, his coach sat down beside him and said, "I'm glad you didn't quit when I was pushing you so hard. There is a reason we train so hard. It makes us better." David then understood that the coach wasn't harassing him. He was training him to be a better player.

There are times when it's okay to push. We all need good life coaches with the right amount of compassion and experience. And at times, we are all called to be that coach for someone else. We can all be a better version of ourselves with the correct combination of love and endurance. Are you laying it all on the line? Do you take direction well?

161

Speak Blessings Over Others

Rather, he must be hospitable, one who loves what is good,
who is self-controlled, upright, holy and disciplined.
TITUS 1:8

It was a chilly Colorado evening as several families sat around the campfire. They looked at me with confusion as I explained that we were going to take turns speaking a blessing over our children. I gave them some examples and said they could also share that "special something" that they see in their child. We were off to a slow start, but it eventually picked up as the parents shared their hopes and dreams for their children. They pointed out their talents with encouragement and affirmation. As they publicly prayed for their families one-by-one, the Spirit moved us into an intense time of worship and praise. Mothers were hugging their children, fathers were crying, and the kids seemed to be very happy. It was the first time that some of them had ever heard a parent speak about them in that way. It was all because we allowed ourselves to open up and speak a blessing over those we held most dear.

But we are to speak this type of blessing over others as well. Our words hold power when we let people know that they are noticed, appreciated, and cared for. Have you used your words to bless someone today? Do you encourage others to be holy through your life and ministry?

162

Eyewitness Encounter: "I Had No Idea What God Was Doing"

"Give, and it will be given to you. A good measure, pressed down, shaken together and running over, will be poured into your lap. For with the measure you use it, it will be measured to you."

LUKE 6:38

One of our college students was working on a school project about our city food bank. She felt like our church should join in these efforts by providing emergency help for our neighbors. She said, "I'm too busy right now to lead this type of project, but I would love to help someone." I liked the idea, but I didn't know of anyone who could lead this with her. Our church had never taken on this type of ministry. The following week, a couple who had recently retired to our area came to ask me if there was any ministry they could help out with. I told them about the food giveaway idea, and they said, "Sounds good. We'll do it." They, along with the college student, proceeded to develop an amazing program. We began with no funding and no space to operate. But soon we discovered the perfect room to store food that was fitted with sturdy shelving from a business that was closing its office. We made a simple plea for funds to get us started. Two years later, they have never lacked the funds or volunteers to provide food for our monthly distribution to 75–100 families. We went in blind, but God showed the way. When He wants something done, we just have to obey and watch Him provide!

—Alan, Senior Pastor

163

Spiritual Nudge: Jean-Pierre De Caussade on No Bounds

"I will surely bless you and make your descendants as numerous as the stars in the sky and as the sand on the seashore. Your descendants will take possessions of the cities of their enemies."

GENESIS 22:17

If God's purpose prescribes for me vocal prayers, loving sentiments, insight into the mysteries, I must love the silence and bareness which a life of faith inspires in others. But for myself, I must take use of my duty to the present and by it unite myself to God. I must not, like the quietists, reduce all religion to a denial of any specific action, despising all other means, since what makes perfection is God's order, and the means he ordains is best for the soul. No, we must set not bounds or limits or shape to the will of God.

We must accept any way he chooses to communicate with us and respect any way it pleases him to unite himself to others. Thus, simple souls have but one general way, though specific and different in each one, which makes up the diversity of the mystical experience.[28]

28. Richard J. Foster & James Bryan Smith, ed., *Devotional Classics: Selected Readings for Individuals and Groups* (New York, New York, HarperOne, 2005). Page 203.

164

Bible Wisdom: Paul on Doing Good

From Galatians 6:1–10

Brothers and sisters, if someone is caught in a sin, you who live by the Spirit should restore that person gently. But watch yourselves, or you also may be tempted. Carry each other's burdens, and in this way you will fulfill the law of Christ. If anyone thinks they are something when they are not, they deceive themselves. Each one should test their own actions. Then they can take pride in themselves alone, without comparing themselves to someone else, for each one should carry their own load. Nevertheless, the one who receives instruction in the word should share all goods things with their instructor.

Do not be deceived: God cannot be mocked. A man reaps what he sows. Whoever sows to please their flesh, from the flesh will reap destruction; whoever sows to please the Spirit, from the Spirit will reap eternal life. Let us not become weary in doing good, for at the proper time we will reap a harvest if we do not give up. Therefore, as we have opportunity, let us do good to all people, especially to those who belong to the family of believers.

165
Toxic People

I urge you, brothers and sisters, to watch out for those who cause divisions and put obstacles in your way that are contrary to the teaching you have learned. Keep away from them.
ROMANS 16:17

Wow. I'm sure we all have a list of people who we would label as "toxic." It doesn't matter where we live, work, or play—there are always folks who can drain the energy right out of us through negativity and doubt. Some are obvious in spreading their toxic vibe. But most of the time, they are subtle and calculating. You know the type. It's the woman who consistently shows up to help but always rolls her eyes at every suggestion or comment. Or the man who says he will support your efforts but instead makes jokes about your abilities. They use tools like gossip and arrogance to slowly sabotage your efforts. They cast doubt in the minds of others through their words and attitudes.

Sometimes we must simply endure and let our good work stand on its own. But there are other times when it becomes necessary to remove toxic people from our lives. Through it all, we must remember that our goal is to help people connect with God. We do not volunteer for personal gain or acknowledgment. But we serve a God who knows all and sees all. He will give us the strength to endure and the wisdom to make necessary changes. Do you volunteer with toxic people? Have you devoted your situation to God?

166

The Wisdom of God

But the wisdom that comes from heaven is first of all pure;
then peace-loving, considerate, submissive, full of
mercy and good fruit, impartial and sincere.

JAMES 3:17

We often confuse wisdom with knowledge. But there is a huge difference. We can hold all the knowledge in the world but still not know what to do with it. Knowledge is good and it's an admirable pursuit, but true wisdom comes from God. Only God can open our hearts and minds with insight and creativity. Our lightbulb moments are the result of God's creativity merging with our feeble knowledge. Then we are able to see things differently. And it is in these moments that our humanity comes alive. We are sparked by a thought. We suddenly "see" a solution that was right in front of us the whole time. Or maybe our hearts are softened by a moment of compassion. Wisdom is also evident when we step out in faith and live for God.

Don't let your level of knowledge be your guide. Instead, open yourself up to God, who will impart wisdom into the life you are living for Him. He wants us to make good choices and spread reconciliation to the world. It is His desire for us to share in this process with Him. But we must first recognize God as our source of wisdom.

167

Praise Him in the Storm

The fear of the LORD is the beginning of wisdom; all who follow his precepts have good understanding. To him belongs eternal praise.
PSALM 111:10

I love thunderstorms. I grew up in the South, and we used to have massive storms with warm rain, dramatic lightening, and booming thunder. As a child, these storms used to scare me. I would run and snuggle up next to my mom, claiming that I was cold or sleepy. But she knew better. As I grew, I began to lose my fear of the storms. I even began to enjoy them. If there was no lightening, we would occasionally go outside and run and play in the rain. I can even remember a fun basketball game or two in the middle of a downpour. But I had to endure many storms before I got to that point.

It's the same in life. The storms that we will face seem so dangerous and scary. They never come at a convenient time, and they disrupt our plans. But we must remember that they will eventually run their course and come to an end. It's what we do during the storms that can make all the difference. Do we run to God for comfort and security? Or do we lash out in anger and bitterness? One path will make us stronger while the other will leave lasting damage. Choosing our plan before the storm will result in a better outcome when we're faced with dramatic lightening and booming thunder. How does your relationship with God shape how you understand your world? Are you able to praise Him during the storms of life?

168
Stay Humble

*Humble yourselves, therefore, under God's mighty hand,
that he may lift you up in due time.*
1 PETER 5:6

Lessons in humility are often harder than lessons in patience. We are taught throughout childhood that we are special and, with enough hard work, we can be anything we want to be. We study, work hard, and try to be the best version of ourselves. As teens, we face stiff competition from our peers. We learn quickly to brag about our personal accomplishments to get ahead. Once we finally have a college diploma and a good job, we feel proud to have achieved society's definition of success. But God has called us to be humble. This is no easy task. It is difficult to try and separate our true worth from the worldly things that make us feel valued. And the only way to see things clearly is to fully embrace God as our source of worth and value. Through His example on the cross, we will find that a life of humility, service, and love is the only path to true peace and success.

169
Eyewitness Encounter: "Double Down"

*And the peace of God, which transcends all understanding,
will guard your hearts and your minds in Christ Jesus.*
PHILIPPIANS 4:7

I've worked in youth ministry for the last ten years of my life. But the last few years of ministry have felt so tiring to me. At times it has been hard to avoid feeling overwhelmed and discouraged. Being tired is a dangerous place to be in ministry because it can deceive us into thinking that our only option is to run away. But during one of my quiet times, this question entered into my mind: "Am I tired *of* ministry, or am I tired *from* ministry?" If the former is true, then it's fair to ask where God wants to take me next. But if the latter is true, then it's time to examine my life and find ways to get the rest and healing that my soul needs.

As I wrestled with that question, I began identifying things that were robbing me of my joy in ministry. I also rediscovered the things about ministry that I truly was excited about. These things had been so hard to see in the midst of discouragement. I've learned that being tired doesn't necessarily mean it's time to jump ship. Instead, it's time to enter into that realm where the peace of God can heal and restore me, allowing me to continue on in my journey.

—Trey, Youth Pastor

170

Spiritual Nudge:
Jon Woolman on Dwelling in Humility

Many, LORD my God, are the wonders you have done, the things you planned for us. None can compare with you; were I to speak and tell of your deeds, they would be too many to declare.

PSALM 40:5

First, my dear friends, dwell in humility and take heed that no views of outward gain get too deep hold of you, that so your eyes being single to the Lord, you may be preserved in the way of safety.

Where people let loose their minds after the love of outward things and are more engaged in pursuing the profits and seeking the friendships of this world than to be inwardly acquainted with the way of true peace, such walk in a vain shadow while the true comfort of life is wanting. Their examples are often hurtful to others, and their treasures thus collected do many times prove dangerous snares to their children.

But where people are sincerely devoted to follow Christ and dwell under the influence of his Holy Spirit, their stability and firmness through a divine blessing is at times like dew on the tender plants round about them, and the weightiness of their spirits secretly works on the minds of others.[29]

171

Bible Wisdom: Moses on Courage

FROM DEUTERONOMY 31:1–8

Then Moses went out and spoke these words to all Israel: "I am now a hundred and twenty years old and I am no longer able to lead you. The LORD has said to me, 'You shall not cross the Jordan.' The LORD your God himself will cross over ahead of you. He will destroy these nations before you, and you will take possession of their land. Joshua also will cross over ahead of you, as the LORD said.

"And the LORD will do to them what he did to Sihon and Og, the kings of the Amorites, whom he destroyed along with their land. The LORD will deliver them to you, and you must do to them all that I have commanded you. Be strong and courageous. Do not be afraid or terrified because of them, for the LORD your God goes with you; he will never leave you nor forsake you."

Then Moses summoned Joshua and said to him in the presence of all

29. John Woolman *The Journal of John Woolman,* Edited by Frederick B. Tolles (New York, New York, Corinth, 1961).

Israel, "Be strong and courageous, for you must go with this people into the land that the LORD swore to their ancestors to give them, and you must divide it among them as their inheritance. The LORD himself goes before you and will be with you; he will never leave you nor forsake you. Do not be afraid; do not be discouraged."

172

Am I Making a Difference?

No discipline seems pleasant at the time, but painful.
Later on, however, it produces a harvest of righteousness
and peace for those who have been trained by it.
HEBREWS 12:11

My father used to drive the church bus every Sunday morning. He spent Saturdays visiting the most extreme neighborhoods, letting people know that they were invited to church. Then, rain or shine, he would drive a bus that was held together by duct tape and zip ties, picking up anyone who wanted to go to church. One day he came across a rough teen boy named Rick who thought he was too cool for school. But the next day Rick was standing by the road waiting for the church bus. For many weeks, he would come to church while maintaining a cool-guy distance from the others. Many thought he was too rough around the edges. Some claimed that he was just using the church bus as a ride into town. But several weeks later, Rick brought some of his younger brothers and sisters with him. Eventually, his entire family began to attend our church. Today, Rick's entire family are believers who faithfully serve in their churches.

God works in mysterious ways. Even when we don't think someone is listening, they are soaking in every word. We give and give and give without knowing if we are helping anyone. Trust that God is at work.

We can't always see what He is doing. But if we remain obedient and faithful, we sometimes get to see the results. We are always making a difference when we are doing the work of the Lord. Have you seen the fruits of your labor? How do you handle it when you don't?

173

His Is Our Hope

Be joyful in hope, patient in affliction, faithful in prayer.
ROMANS 12:12

Hope is a powerful thing. It can help children thrive despite horrible situations. It can give a victim the strength to hold on for one more day. It can help a man survive brutal abuses. It can change the course of entire nations. But hope is more than just wishful thinking. Real hope is rooted in God. Recognizing Him as our source and sustainer floods even the most desperate situations with hope. Yes, we live in a broken world. Yes, we sometimes endure intense pain. But hope for a better future helps us fix our eyes on the destiny Christ promised us. The day will come when we are finally separated from the brokenness of this world and reunited with our Creator. This is why we keep putting one foot in front of the other. He gives us the strength to carry on.

174

Be Strong and Courageous

"Be strong and courageous. Do not be afraid or terrified because of them, for the LORD your God goes with you; he will never leave you nor forsake you."

DEUTERONOMY 31:6

Inner strength doesn't always come easily. Sure, there are folks who are born with a strong will. But for most of us, inner strength is a lifelong pursuit full of trial and error that garners us confidence and wisdom. Thankfully, the Bible tells us that we don't have to rely on our own strength. As the children of God, His strength and courage flow through our every breath. When we suddenly have the correct answer or feel calm in the face of adversity, this is the work of His Spirit. So when you find yourself feeling weak and scared, take a moment to seek God. Praise Him and recognize His Lordship in your life. He is the only source of strength and courage that we can truly trust. Where does your strength come from?

175
Just Love Them

And now these three remain: faith, hope and love.
But the greatest of these is love.
1 CORINTHIANS 13:13

Do you ever feel totally confused by another person's actions? We unknowingly come to expect certain behavior from the people in our lives, and when we are blindsided by an uncharacteristic comment or harsh tone, we typically react in self-defense and shock. We may immediately begin to ask ourselves if we did something wrong. And a little self-examination can be a good thing, but the reason behind someone's unusual attitude might still elude us. Our next thoughts should be full of compassion and support. Most of the time we have no idea what the other person is going through. We may not know that they are having a hard time at home or at work or with a relative. Maybe they are processing some bad news. Even the best excuse doesn't make it okay for people to lash out at one another, but likewise, even the worst offense doesn't give us permission to respond in kind.

Unexpected emotions can make our times of service to others very difficult. It's not uncommon to question why we are spending our time volunteering when we are working with difficult people. But as God's love flows through us, we must remember to just love them. Through the good and the bad, we are called to be a people of compassion and empathy. Remembering the grace that God first showed us makes it possible.

176

Eyewitness Encounter: "It Was Worth It"

For the LORD God is a sun and shield; the LORD
bestows favor and honor; no good thing does he
withhold from those whose walk is blameless.
PSALM 84:11

It was finally here. Opening night of the community Easter play. We had held auditions, practiced, painted the sets, positioned the lights, advertised, sold tickets, made costumes, rented an auditorium, and chose the songs. Over fifty people were in the cast, and more than that worked behind the scenes to help pull together all the details. It was finally coming together, and I was left shaking in my shoes. As the director, I was praying that it would all be worthwhile. Not just because we wanted to put on a good show, but because we were telling the amazing story of Christ's resurrection. We were trying to do a good thing. And there were folks in the audience who may never hear of this gift again. We had to get it right.

I ran back and forth, calling directions through my headset. But as the stone was rolled away, I paused to check out the audience. I gazed out upon face after face that appeared spellbound by the story. There were no dry eyes in the room. People cried, raised their hands in praise, and some even stood and clapped as He rose from the grave. As the Holy Spirit filled the room, I knew that it had all been worth it. We had given our best, and He touched the lives of so many that night. I am eternally grateful to have been a part of this life-changing night.

—**Bonnie, Play Director**

177

Spiritual Nudge:
Henri J. M. Nouwen on Radical Love

*"I have set you an example that you
should do as I have done for you."*
JOHN 13:15

"After washing His disciples' feet, Jesus says, 'I have given you an example so that you may copy what I have done to you' (John 13:15). After giving Himself as food and drink, He says, 'Do this in remembrance of me' (Luke 22:19). Jesus calls us to continue His mission of revealing the perfect love of God in this world. He calls us to total self-giving. He does not want us to keep anything for ourselves. Rather, He wants our love to be as full, as radical, and as complete as His own. He wants us to bend ourselves to the ground and touch the places in each other that most need washing. He also wants us to say to each other, 'Eat of me and drink of me.' By this complete mutual nurturing, He wants us to become one body and one spirit, united by the love of God."[30]

30. Henri J. Nouwen, *Show Me the Way* (New York, New York, Crossroads Publishing Company, 1995) pp. 130-131.

178

Bible Wisdom: Christ on Persecution

FROM JOHN 15:18–25

"If the world hates you, keep in mind that it hated me first. If you belonged to the world, it would love you as its own. As it is, you do not belong to the world, but I have chosen you out of the world. That is why the world hates you. Remember what I told you: 'A servant is not greater than his master.' If they persecuted me, they will persecute you also. If they obeyed my teaching, they will obey yours also. They will treat you this way because of my name, for they do not know the one who sent me. If I had not come and spoken to them, they would not be guilty of sin; but now they have no excuse for their sin. Whoever hates me hates my Father as well. If I had not done among them the works no one else did, they would not be guilty of sin. As it is, they have seen, and yet they have hated both me and my Father. But this is to fulfill what is written in their Law: 'They hated me without reason.'"

179

My Prayer of Binding and Loosing: Praying in God's Authority

"Truly I tell you, whatever you bind on earth will be bound in heaven, and whatever you loose on earth will be loosed in heaven."
MATTHEW 18:18

Jesus tells us in this verse that we have authority in His name.

Yet this type of prayer is effective only if our request is in line with God's Word and His laws, and we draw its power from God Himself—not from our own desires and abilities. So a prayer of binding and loosing should never be entered into casually. It's serious business!

For example, we should never attempt to "bind" a rival soccer team to lose the state tournament or "loose" our boss to give us a big promotion.

We can, however, bind evil spirits that are attacking someone or loose angelic spirits to work on our behalf in those areas where God has already promised us results. When we pray in this manner, God affirms it in heaven and puts His seal of approval on our prayer.

But again, understand that binding and loosing has to be based on the authority God has granted us in scripture, not on our own desires.

My Prayer of Protection and Deliverance:

_____
_____
_____
_____
_____
_____

180

My Prayers: "Lord, Protect and Deliver Us. . ."

*One of you routs a thousand, because the LORD
your God fights for you, just as he promised.*
JOSHUA 23:10

My Prayer of Protection and Deliverance for My Family:

_____

_____

_____

My Prayer of Protection and Deliverance for My Friends:

_____

_____

_____

My Prayer of Protection and Deliverance for My Church:

_____

_____

_____

My Prayer of Protection and Deliverance for My Workplace:

_____

_____

_____

Also available from goTandem

gotandemresources.com